Vanessa-Ann's
Victorian
Cross-Stitch

The Vanessa-Ann Collection

Owner

Jo Packham

Staff

Trice Boerens

Gaylene Byers

Holly Fuller

Cherie Hanson

Susan Jorgensen

Margaret Shields Marti

Jackie McCowen

Barbara Milburn

Pamela Randall

Jennifer Roberts

Nancy Whitley

Designers

Terrece Beesley

Trice Boerens

Florence Stacey

Photographer

Ryne Hazen

The Vanessa-Ann Collection extends its thanks to Penelope Hammons in Layton, Utah, Ned and Maggie Favero in Coalville, Utah, and Jo Packham in Ogden, Utah, for the use of their beautiful homes for photography. Their trust and cooperation are greatly appreciated.

*D*irecting the style and photography for **Vanessa-Ann's Victorian Cross-Stitch** came very easily for Jo Packham, owner of The Vanessa-Ann Collection, because Victoriana and cross-stitch are such an essential part of her world. She simply envisioned a collection of elegant and sophisticated works that was dear to her heart.

Having met through a mutual friend, Jo Packham and Terrece Beesley started The Vanessa-Ann Collection nearly fifteen years ago. As the primary artist for this and most other publications from the company, Terrece is a master of subtle colors and a variety of styles and subjects. Since the days when they worked at their respective kitchen tables in Ogden, Utah, Jo and Terrece have published some 200 cross-stitch, quilting, crochet, and crafts titles. Together they built a company that set a standard in the industry for its innovative ideas in needlework.

Today, with the changes in each of their families, Terrece works from her home in Ohio as a freelance artist and Jo owns and oversees Vanessa-Ann's day-to-day operations. In the pages of this book, the talents of both women are showcased.

This book is sincerely dedicated to all of us who,
no matter how old we become,
still believe in the magic and the possibility
of childhood dreams.

Library of Congress Catalog Number: 93-086048
Hardcover ISBN: 0-8487-0768-0
Softcover ISBN: 0-8487-1425-3
Manufactured in the United States of America
First Printing 1993

Editor-in-Chief: Nancy J. Fitzpatrick
Senior Crafts Editor: Susan Ramey Wright
Senior Editor, Editorial Services: Olivia Kindig Wells
Director of Manufacturing: Jerry Higdon
Art Director: James Boone

Vanessa-Ann's Victorian Cross-Stitch
from The Joys of Cross-Stitch Series

Editor: Laurie Pate Sewell
Assistant Editor: Shannon Leigh Sexton
Editorial Assistant: Janica Lynn York
Copy Editor: Susan Smith Cheatham
Copy Assistant: Leslee Rester Johnson
Production Manager: Rick Litton
Associate Production Manager: Theresa L. Beste
Production Assistant: Marianne Jordan
Designer: Eleanor Cameron
Illustrators: Kelly Davis, Karen Tindall Tillery
Senior Production Designer: Larry Hunter
Publishing Systems Administrator: Rick Tucker

Table of Contents

Introduction

*S*tep back in time to a world
of grace and elegance. The nostalgic
designs in **Vanessa-Ann's
Victorian Cross-Stitch** capture
the spirit of the era with lush
colors and charming motifs.
Each chapter is filled with projects
from the heart and for the home.
Embellish gifts for friends or
enhance their homes (and yours!)
with lovely and detailed items.
These original designs from The
Vanessa-Ann Collection create a
stylish Victorian look by bringing
together floral motifs, lace, velvet,
and ribbon. As you stitch through
each chapter, welcome the return
of finery from a bygone age.

The Home Collection

*H*ome is a welcome
refuge for family and friends.
It is a place where we are free to
be ourselves, where we can love
and be loved. To add an extra-
special warmth to your home,
decorate rooms with bellpulls and
afghans, chair cushions and
footstools. Each handmade design
will be cherished by all.

Iris Afghan

SAMPLE

Stitched on Vanessa-Ann Afghan Weave 18 over 2 threads, the finished design size is 5" x 4⅞". The fabric was cut 48" x 58". (The width measurement includes 7 whole blocks with ½ block on each side, and the length measurement includes 8 whole blocks with ½ block on each end.) The stitching area of each woven block is 88 x 88 threads. Begin stitching the motif in the center of each block and repeat 7 times across 1 end of the afghan. See Suppliers for afghan material.

FABRICS	DESIGN SIZES
Aida 11	3⅞" x 4"
Aida 14	3" x 3⅛"
Aida 18	2½" x 2½"
Hardanger 22	1⅞" x 2"

MATERIALS

Completed cross-stitch on Vanessa-Ann Afghan Weave 18
Overture yarn, 3 skeins #V93 (see Suppliers)
¾ yard (45"-wide) purple fabric; matching thread

DIRECTIONS

1. Trim design piece to 45" x 54". Using 1 strand of Overture yarn and referring to photo, sew running stitches at ½" intervals around each woven square on afghan.

2. From purple fabric, cut 2¼"-wide bias strips, piecing as needed to equal 5½ yards.

3. Bind edges with bias strip, using ½" seam and mitering corners.

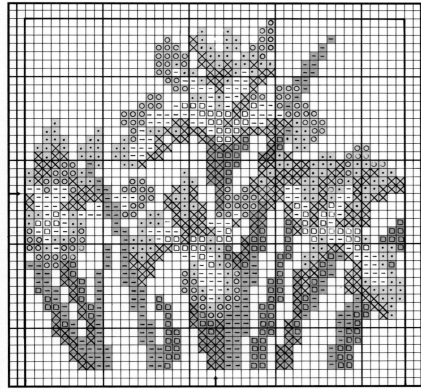

Stitch Count: 44 x 42

Anchor		DMC (used for sample)	
	Step 1:	Cross-stitch (3 strands)	
891	−	676	Old Gold-lt.
323	□	722	Orange Spice-lt. (2 strands)
891		676	Old Gold-lt. (1 strand)
95	·	554	Violet-lt.
110	○	208	Lavender-vy. dk.
119	✕	333	Blue Violet-dk.
214	−	368	Pistachio Green-lt.
215	▣	320	Pistachio Green-med.
878	✕	501	Blue Green-dk.

Flowery Footstool

SAMPLE
Stitched on driftwood Belfast Linen 32 over 2 threads, the finished design size is 5" x 2¼" for 1 motif. The fabric was cut 46" x 8". The number of motifs varies according to the size of the footstool used. The sample shown is stitched to a 16" x 12" oval footstool and uses 8 motifs. The bold lines on the graph indicate repeats.

FABRICS	DESIGN SIZES (for 1 motif)
Aida 11	7¼" x 3⅛"
Aida 14	5¾" x 2½"
Aida 18	4½" x 2"
Hardanger 22	3⅝" x 1⅝"

MATERIALS

Completed cross-stitch on driftwood Belfast Linen 32; matching thread
16" x 12" oval padded and upholstered footstool
1½ yards (⅛"-wide) silk ribbon in each color: burgundy, brown, green
1¼ yards (⅝"-wide) upholstery trim with tassels
Large-eyed needle
Hot-glue gun and glue sticks

DIRECTIONS

1. With design centered, trim design piece to 3½" x 44". Turn long edges under ¼"; press. Beginning with 1 end of strip at center back of footstool, align bottom edge of strip with base of footstool. Slipstitch bottom edge of design piece to footstool cover. Smooth design piece snugly against footstool, keeping tension on fabric even, and slipstitch top edge of design piece to footstool cover. Turn remaining end under, overlapping ends; slipstitch ends together.

2. To embellish, thread needle with brown ribbon and knot 1 end. Draw ribbon through footstool cover along top edge of design piece, looping and twisting ribbon loosely and knotting where desired. Do not draw ribbon tight (see photo). To secure end of ribbon, draw through footstool cover and knot; trim excess. Repeat with burgundy and green ribbons, weaving each color loosely through other colors and knotting where desired.

3. Glue upholstery trim along bottom edge of design piece, covering slipstitching.

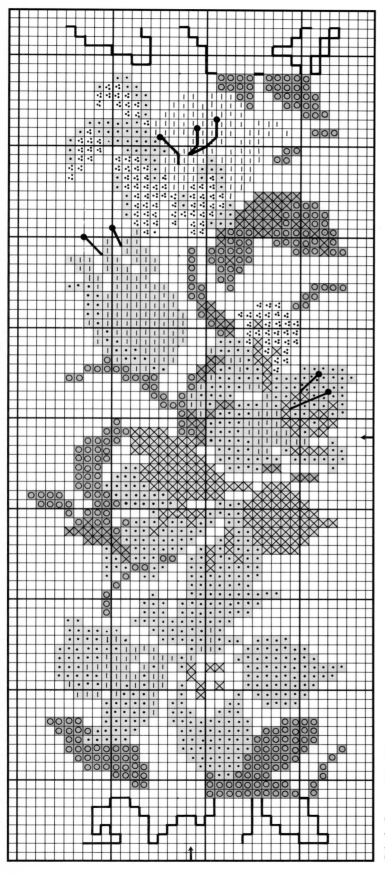

Stitch Count: 80 x 35

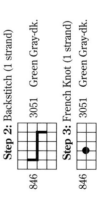

Step 2: Backstitch (1 strand)

846 — 3051 Green Gray-dk.

Step 3: French Knot (1 strand)

	●	

846 3051 Green Gray-dk.

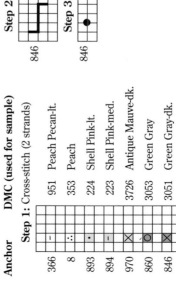

Anchor   DMC (used for sample)

Step 1: Cross-stitch (2 strands)

Anchor		DMC	
366	-	951	Peach Pecan-lt.
8	∴	353	Peach
893	•	224	Shell Pink-lt.
894	ı	223	Shell Pink-med.
970	✕	3726	Antique Mauve-dk.
860	◐	3053	Green Gray
846	⊠	3051	Green Gray-dk.

Alphabet Bellpull

SAMPLE

Stitched on oatmeal Floba 18 over 2 threads, the finished design size is 8½" x 20". The fabric was cut 15" x 26½". See Suppliers for bellpull hardware set.

FABRICS	DESIGN SIZES
Aida 11	6⅞" x 16⅜"
Aida 14	5½" x 12⅞"
Aida 18	4¼" x 10"
Hardanger 22	3½" x 8⅛"

MATERIALS

Completed cross-stitch on oatmeal Floba 18; matching thread
1 (9¾" x 26½") piece of unstitched Floba 18 for backing
½ yard of tan satin fabric
1½ yards (¼") cording
1 (9¾" x 26½") piece of flannel for lining
Dressmaker's pen
1 (10½"-wide) bellpull hardware set

DIRECTIONS

All seam allowances are ¼".

1. With design centered, trim design piece to 9¾" x 26½". From tan satin, cut 1¼"-wide bias strips, piecing as needed to equal 1½ yards. Make 1½ yards of corded piping.

2. Cut piping in half. With right sides facing and raw edges aligned, stitch 1 piece of piping to 1 long edge of design piece, tapering ends slightly. Repeat for other long edge.

3. Stack flannel lining, design piece (right side up), and unstitched Floba backing. Stitch together, sewing along stitching line of piping and leaving 1 end open for turning. Trim corners and turn. Turn under seam allowance and slipstitch opening closed. Press.

4. With dressmaker's pen, mark fold lines on front of bellpull 2" above and 2" below design. Slip ends of bellpull around posts of hardware and fold fabric to back of bellpull along marked lines. Slipstitch ends to backing.

(Top Section)

Overture Yarn (used for sample)

Step 1: Cross-stitch (1 strand)

V49	Carmels
V58	Spices
V96	Bayberries
V33	Brandywine

Step 2: Backstitch (1 strand)

839 Beige Brown-dk.
DMC Floss

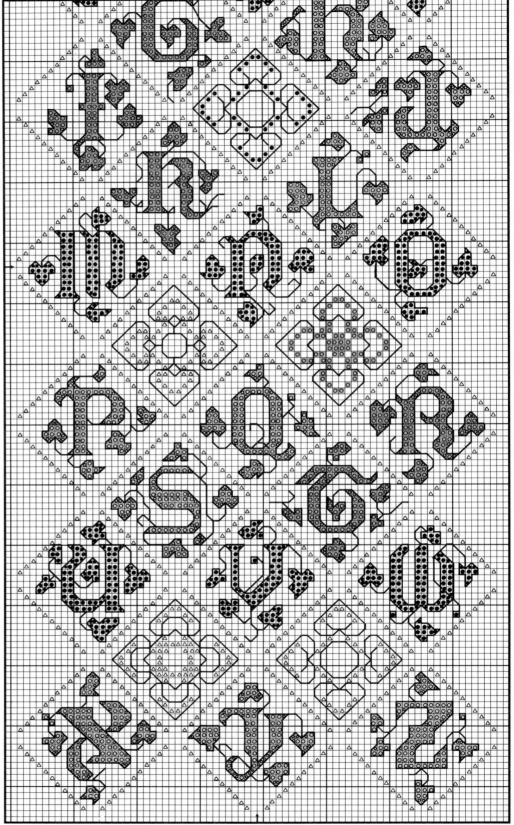

Stitch Count: 76 x 180

(Bottom Section)

Sylvan Sprites Dresser Tray

SAMPLE

Stitched on cream Belfast Linen 32 over 2 threads, the finished design size is 10½" x 6⅜". The fabric was cut 17" x 13". The design piece was placed in an antique dresser tray with a 12" x 17" oval glass opening.

FABRICS	DESIGN SIZES
Aida 11	14⅞" x 8¾"
Aida 14	11⅝" x 6⅞"
Aida 18	9" x 5⅜"
Hardanger 22	7⅜" x 4⅜"

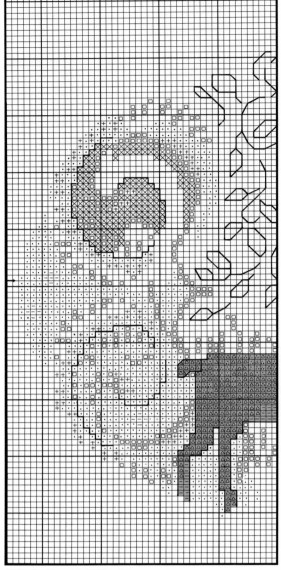

Stitch Count: 163 x 96

Anchor		DMC (used for sample)	
		Step 1: Cross-stitch (2 strands)	
881		945	Peach Beige
4146		754	Peach-lt.
8		761	Salmon-lt.
869		3743	Antique Violet-vy. lt.
95		554	Violet-lt.
98		553	Violet-med.
118		340	Blue Violet-med.
158		775	Baby Blue-vy. lt.
159		827	Blue-vy. lt.
160		813	Blue-lt.
121		794	Cornflower Blue-lt.
940		792	Cornflower Blue-dk.
214		966	Baby Green-med.
213		504	Blue Green-lt.
876		502	Blue Green
878		501	Blue Green-dk.
885		739	Tan-ultra vy. lt.
942		738	Tan-vy. lt.
882		3773	Pecan-vy. lt.
914		3772	Pecan-med.
379		840	Beige Brown-med.
397		762	Pearl Gray-vy. lt.
8581		646	Beaver Gray-dk.
		Step 2: Backstitch (1 strand)	
876		502	Blue Green (vines)
236		3799	Pewter Gray-vy. dk. (all else)
		Step 3: French Knot (1 strand)	
236		3799	Pewter Gray-vy. dk.

Elegant Table Scarf

SAMPLE

Stitched on black Dublin 25 over 2 threads, the finished design size is 25" x 15¾". The fabric was cut 31" x 22". The graph shows the top half of the design. Rotate the graph to stitch the bottom half of the design.

FABRICS	DESIGN SIZES
Aida 11	28½" x 17⅞"
Aida 14	22⅜" x 14⅛"
Aida 18	17⅜" x 11"
Hardanger 22	14¼" x 9"

MATERIALS

Completed cross-stitch on black Dublin Linen 25; matching thread
½ yard of print fabric in colors to match design for backing
2¾ yards (2"-wide) black flat lace
2½ yards (⅝"-wide) gold/black flat trim
DMC floss, 2 skeins each #437, #3721, #3778
Balger blending filament, 1 spool each #021, #013

DIRECTIONS

1. With design centered, trim linen to measure 27" x 17¾". Cut backing fabric to match design piece. With right sides facing and raw edges aligned, stitch pieces together around all edges, using ¼" seam and leaving an opening for turning. Turn. Slipstitch opening closed. Press.

2. Beginning at 1 corner, slipstitch lace to top of design piece ¼" from stitched design, mitering corners. Slipstitch trim to top of design piece along edges of stitched design, covering stitched edge of lace.

3. Referring to General Instructions, make 4 (5½") tassels, using ½ skein of each floss color for each tassel and an equal amount of both blending filaments. Tack tassels at each corner of scarf (see photo for placement).

Stitch Count 313 x 197

Anchor   **DMC (used for sample)**

Step 1: Cross-stitch (3 strands DMC +
1 strand Balger blending filament)

337   ⌐3778 Terra Cotta (5 skeins)
      └021 Copper Balger (7 spools)

896   ⌐3721 Shell Pink-dk. (11 skeins)
      └021 Copper Balger

362   ⌐437 Tan-lt. (4 skeins)
      └013 Beige Balger (2 spools)

Fanciful Floral Cushion

SAMPLE
Stitched on blush Linen 28 over 2 threads, the finished design size is 12⅛" x 12⅛". The fabric was cut 22" x 22". Begin stitching so that the bottom edge of the design is 3" to the left of the fabric center. Repeat the motif 3 times, moving clockwise to form a circular pattern. (The bold line on the right side of the graph indicates repeat.) Adjust measurements to accommodate your chair cushion.

FABRICS	DESIGN SIZES
Aida 11	15½" x 15½"
Aida 14	12⅛" x 12⅛"
Aida 18	9½" x 9½"
Hardanger 22	7¾" x 7¾"

MATERIALS
Completed cross-stitch on blush Linen 28; matching thread
1 (1¾") covered-button kit
Scrap of blush Linen 28
1 (15"-diameter) piece of ½"-thick pressboard
1 (18"-diameter) piece of extra-loft batting
Fabric glue
Transparent tape
1 (14"-diameter) piece of mat board
Staple gun

DIRECTIONS
1. Cover button with linen scrap as directed in kit. Center design piece right side up on batting. Tack button in place at center of cross-stitch design through both layers.

2. Using fabric glue, cover 1 side of pressboard with batting and design piece, folding excess over edges of pressboard; tape in place.

3. Turn cushion over and place mat board in center. Using staple gun, staple mat board in place around edges to cover raw edges of fabric.

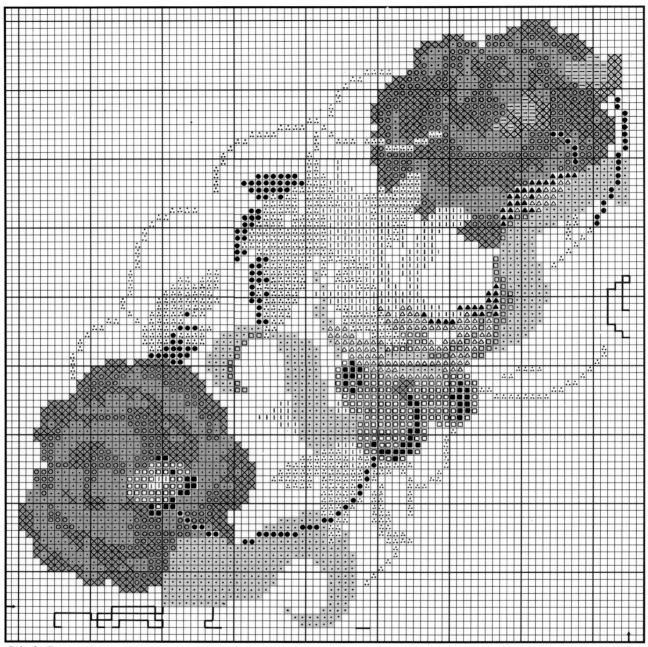

Stitch Count: 170 x 170

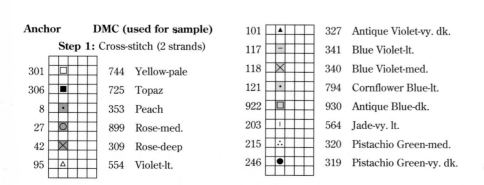

Anchor		DMC (used for sample)
Step 1: Cross-stitch (2 strands)		
301	□	744 Yellow-pale
306	■	725 Topaz
8	·	353 Peach
27	◎	899 Rose-med.
42	⊠	309 Rose-deep
95	△	554 Violet-lt.

101	▲	327 Antique Violet-vy. dk.
117	—	341 Blue Violet-lt.
118	⊠	340 Blue Violet-med.
121	·	794 Cornflower Blue-lt.
922	□	930 Antique Blue-dk.
203	❘	564 Jade-vy. lt.
215	∴	320 Pistachio Green-med.
246	●	319 Pistachio Green-vy. dk.

Star-Bright Stocking

SAMPLE

Stitched on cream Aida 14 over 1 thread, the finished design size is 7¾" x 14⅜". The fabric was cut 14" x 21".

FABRICS	DESIGN SIZES
Aida 11	9⅞" x 18⅜"
Aida 18	6" x 11¼"
Hardanger 22	5" x 9⅛"

MATERIALS

Completed cross-stitch on cream Aida 14
½ yard (45"-wide) lavender moire taffeta fabric; matching thread
½ yard of polyester fleece
2 yards (¼"-wide) sheer rose silk ribbon
1½ yards (⅝"-wide) pink wired ribbon
1½ yards (⅝"-wide) lavender wired ribbon
Dressmaker's pen
1 yard (¼") cording

DIRECTIONS

All seam allowances are ¼".

1. To make stocking pattern, use dressmaker's pen to mark design piece ¼" outside design area on all edges. Cut along marks.

2. Using design piece as pattern, cut 3 stocking pieces from taffeta (1 for back and 2 for lining) and 2 stocking pieces from fleece.

Also from taffeta, cut 1 (1¼" x 4½") strip for hanger loop and 1¼"-wide bias strips, piecing as needed to equal 1 yard. Make 1 yard of corded piping. Set aside.

3. To make stocking front, baste 1 fleece piece to wrong side of design piece. With right sides facing and raw edges aligned, stitch piping around sides and bottom of stocking front. To make stocking back, baste remaining fleece piece to wrong side of 1 taffeta piece.

4. To assemble stocking, with right sides facing and raw edges aligned, stitch stocking front to back, sewing along stitching line of piping. Trim fleece from seam allowance. Clip curves and turn.

5. With right sides facing and raw edges aligned, fold hanger in half lengthwise. Stitch long raw edge and turn. With raw ends aligned, fold hanger in half to form loop. With raw edges aligned, baste ends of hanger to right side of stocking back at top corner above heel.

6. To make stocking lining, stitch remaining 2 taffeta pieces together, leaving top edge open and a large opening in side seam above heel. Clip curves. Do not turn. With right sides facing, slide lining over stocking, matching side seams and top edges. Stitch lining to stocking around top edge, securing hanger in seam. Trim fleece from seam allowance. Turn stocking through opening in lining. Slipstitch opening closed. Tuck lining inside stocking.

7. Cut 1 (12") piece of sheer rose silk ribbon. To make bow, fold remaining silk ribbon and other ribbons into loops, leaving long tails. Handling ribbons as 1, tie 12" piece around center of loops. Tack bow to top right corner of stocking. Knot ribbons 1" from ends.

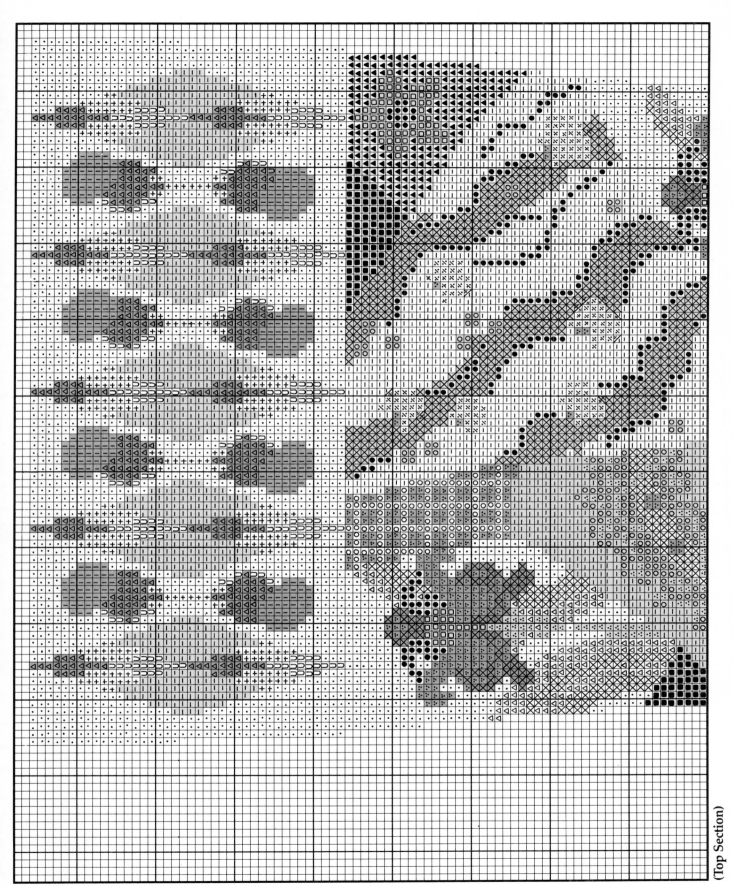

(Top Section)

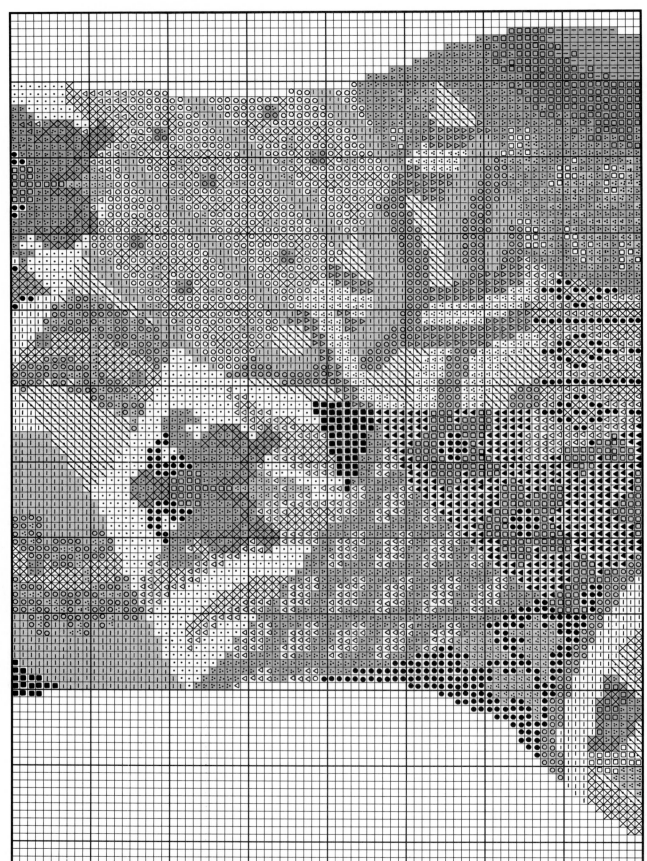

(Middle Section)

Stitch Count: 109 x 202

(Bottom Section)

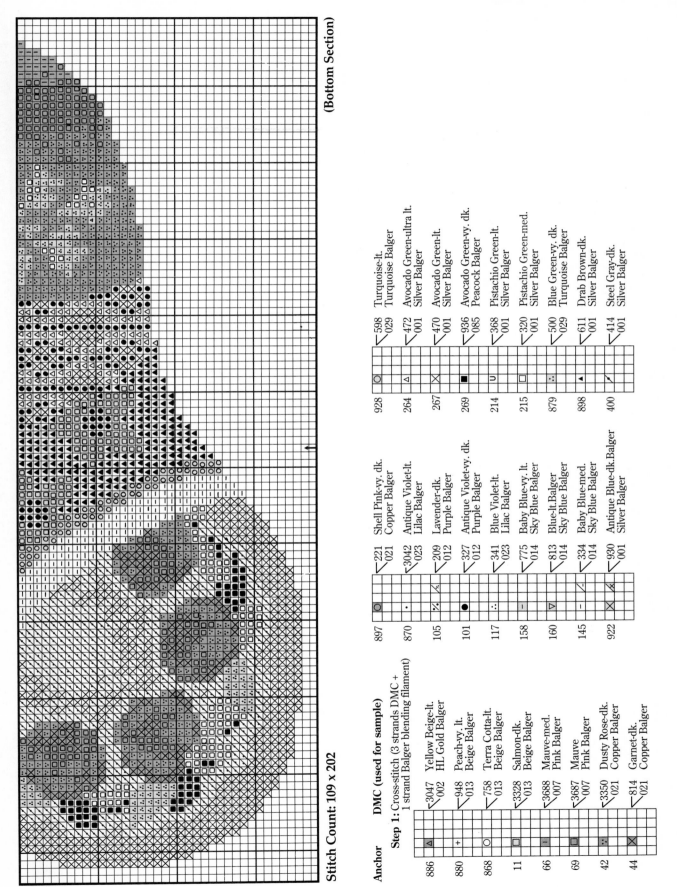

Anchor **DMC (used for sample)**

Step 1: Cross-stitch (3 strands DMC + 1 strand Balger blending filament)

Anchor		DMC		
886	▲	3047/002	Yellow Beige-lt.	HL Gold Balger
880	+	948/013	Peach-vy. lt.	Beige Balger
868	○	758/013	Terra Cotta-lt.	Beige Balger
11	□	3328/013	Salmon-dk.	Beige Balger
66	▬	3688/007	Mauve-med.	Pink Balger
69	▣	3687/007	Mauve	Pink Balger
42	∴	3350/021	Dusty Rose-dk.	Copper Balger
44	✕	814/021	Garnet-dk.	Copper Balger

Anchor		DMC		
897	◉	221/021	Shell Pink-vy. dk.	Copper Balger
870	·	3042/023	Antique Violet-lt.	Lilac Balger
105	⅔	209/012	Lavender-dk.	Purple Balger
101	●	327/012	Antique Violet-vy. dk.	Purple Balger
117	⋮	341/023	Blue Violet-lt.	Lilac Balger
158	−	775/014	Baby Blue-vy. lt.	Sky Blue Balger
160	▷	813/014	Blue-lt.	Sky Blue Balger
145	⁄	334/014	Baby Blue-med.	Sky Blue Balger
922	✕	930/001	Antique Blue-dk. Balger	Silver Balger

Anchor		DMC		
928	◉	598/029	Turquoise-lt.	Turquoise Balger
264	△	472/001	Avocado Green-ultra lt.	Silver Balger
267	✕	470/001	Avocado Green-lt.	Silver Balger
269	■	936/085	Avocado Green-vy. dk.	Peacock Balger
214	∪	368/001	Pistachio Green-lt.	Silver Balger
215	□	320/001	Pistachio Green-med.	Silver Balger
879	∴	500/029	Blue Green-vy. dk.	Turquoise Balger
898	◀	611/001	Drab Brown-dk.	Silver Balger
400	⟋	414/001	Steel Gray-dk.	Silver Balger

Sweet Blossoms

SAMPLE
Stitched on blush Linen 28 over 2 threads, the finished design size is 14⅛" x 9". The fabric was cut 21" x 15". The completed design was placed in an antique table and covered with glass.

FABRICS
DESIGN SIZES

FABRICS	DESIGN SIZES
Aida 11	18" x 11½"
Aida 14	14⅛" x 9"
Aida 18	11" x 7"
Hardanger 22	9" x 5¾"

Anchor		DMC (used for sample)	
	Step 1:	Cross-stitch (2 strands)	
386	+	746	Off White
386	•	746	Off White (1 strand)
4146		754	Peach-lt. (1 strand)
8	−	353	Peach
9	△	760	Salmon
386	•	746	Off White (1 strand)
271		3713	Salmon-vy. lt. (1 strand)
24	−	776	Pink-med.
75	□	962	Wild Rose-med.
76	∴	3731	Dusty Rose-med.
66	○	3688	Mauve-med.
69	✕	3687	Mauve
896	□	3722	Shell Pink
104	△	210	Lavender-med.
98	▲	553	Violet-med.
118	+	340	Blue Violet-med.
214	I	368	Pistachio Green-lt.
215	∴	320	Pistachio Green-med.
242	○	989	Forest Green
244	●	987	Forest Green-dk.
208	•	563	Jade-lt.
210	✕	562	Jade-med.
878	□	501	Blue Green-dk.
879	■	500	Blue Green-vy. dk.
942	+	738	Tan-vy. lt.
362	✕	437	Tan-lt.
914	○	3064	Pecan-lt.

Step 2: Backstitch (1 strand)

69		3687	Mauve (mauve roses)
896		3722	Shell Pink (peach roses)
914		3064	Pecan-lt. (all else)

Stitch Count: 198 x 126

Pillow
Pleasures

*Nothing surpasses
the comfort and luxury of
pillows. Indulge in the elegance
of velvet enhanced with dainty
stitches, or the crisp, clean feel of
linen graced with sophisticated
specialty stitches. Whatever
your pillow pleasure, you'll find
a design to suit your style. So
pamper yourself or a friend with
mounds of uniquely shaped
pillows to add artistry to
any decor.*

39

Shaped Pillows

SAMPLE for Diamond Pillow

Stitched on blush Linen 28 over 2 threads, the finished design size is 8⅛" x 10¾". The fabric was cut 15" x 17".

FABRICS	DESIGN SIZES
Aida 11	10⅜" x 13¾"
Aida 14	8⅛" x 10¾"
Aida 18	6⅜" x 8⅜"
Hardanger 22	5⅛" x 6⅞"

SAMPLE for Heart Pillow

Stitched on blush Linen 28 over 2 threads, the finished design size is 8⅜" x 7⅞". The fabric was cut 15" x 14".

FABRICS	DESIGN SIZES
Aida 11	10¾" x 10"
Aida 14	8⅜" x 7⅞"
Aida 18	6½" x 6⅛"
Hardanger 22	5⅜" x 5"

SAMPLE for Club Pillow

Stitched on blush Linen 28 over 2 threads, the finished design size is 7⅞" x 7⅞". The fabric was cut 14" x 14".

FABRICS	DESIGN SIZES
Aida 11	10" x 10"
Aida 14	7⅞" x 7⅞"
Aida 18	6⅛" x 6⅛"
Hardanger 22	5" x 5"

MATERIALS (for 1 pillow)

Completed cross-stitch on blush Linen 28; matching thread
1 (14" x 18") piece of unstitched blush Linen 28
½ yard (45"-wide) pink fabric; matching thread
1¼ yards (¼") cording
Dressmaker's pen
Polyester stuffing

DIRECTIONS

All seam allowances are ¼".

1. To make pattern, use dressmaker's pen to mark 3" outside stitching on design piece, rounding corners slightly to make shape symmetrical. Cut out along marked lines.

2. Using design piece as pattern, cut 1 shape from unstitched linen for backing and 1 from pink fabric for lining. Also from pink fabric, cut 1¼"-wide bias strips, piecing as needed to equal 1¼ yards. Make corded piping.

3. To make lined pillow front, layer design piece (right side up) on top of pink fabric shape. Zigzag all edges together. Press as needed to keep layers flat.

4. To attach piping, with right sides facing and raw edges aligned, stitch piping to design piece, rounding corners slightly. With right sides facing and raw edges aligned, stitch design piece to pillow back, sewing along stitching line of piping and leaving an opening for turning. Clip curves and turn. Stuff firmly. Slipstitch opening closed.

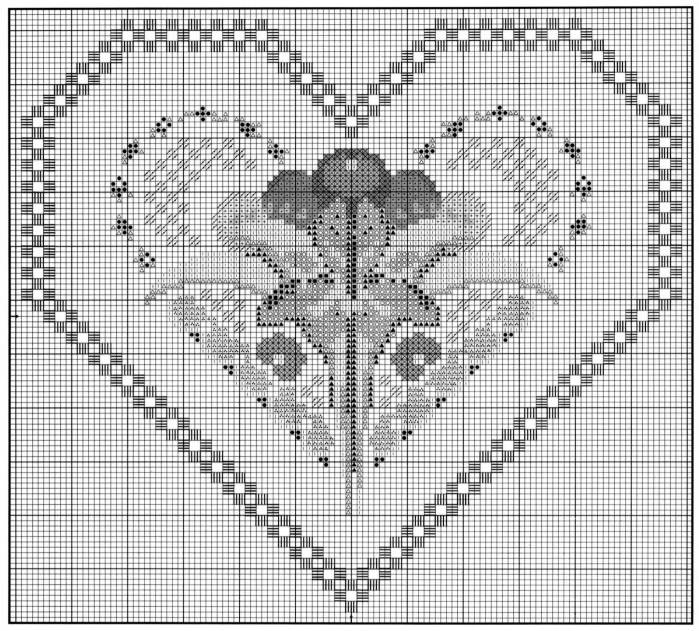

Stitch Count: 118 x 110 (Heart)

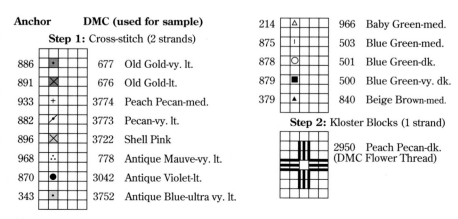

Anchor		DMC (used for sample)
		Step 1: Cross-stitch (2 strands)
886		677 Old Gold-vy. lt.
891		676 Old Gold-lt.
933		3774 Peach Pecan-med.
882		3773 Pecan-vy. lt.
896		3722 Shell Pink
968		778 Antique Mauve-vy. lt.
870		3042 Antique Violet-lt.
343		3752 Antique Blue-ultra vy. lt.

214		966 Baby Green-med.
875		503 Blue Green-med.
878		501 Blue Green-dk.
879		500 Blue Green-vy. dk.
379		840 Beige Brown-med.

Step 2: Kloster Blocks (1 strand)

2950 Peach Pecan-dk.
(DMC Flower Thread)

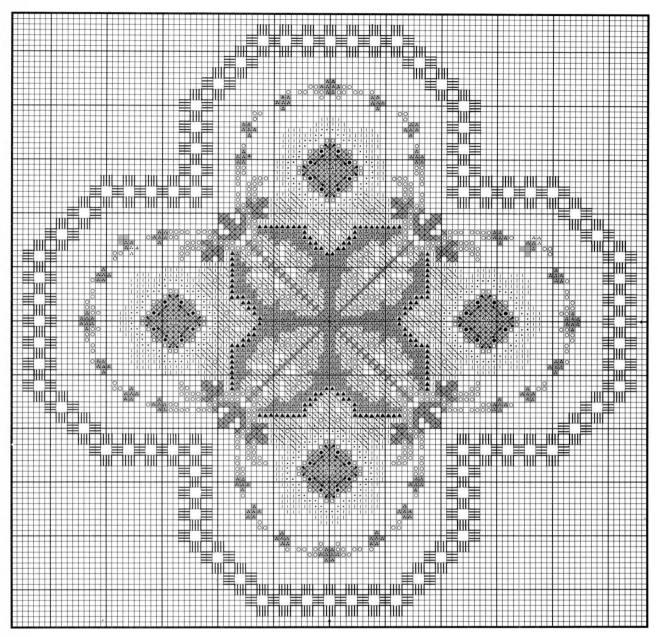

Stitch Count: 110 x 110 (Club)

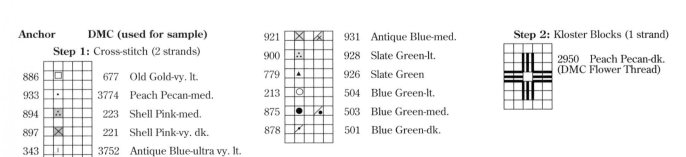

Anchor		DMC (used for sample)
		Step 1: Cross-stitch (2 strands)
886	☐	677 Old Gold-vy. lt.
933	·	3774 Peach Pecan-med.
894	∴	223 Shell Pink-med.
897	☒	221 Shell Pink-vy. dk.
343	ǀ	3752 Antique Blue-ultra vy. lt.

921	☒ ◪	931	Antique Blue-med.
900	∴	928	Slate Green-lt.
779	▲	926	Slate Green
213	○	504	Blue Green-lt.
875	● ◐	503	Blue Green-med.
878	⟋	501	Blue Green-dk.

Step 2: Kloster Blocks (1 strand)

2950 Peach Pecan-dk.
(DMC Flower Thread)

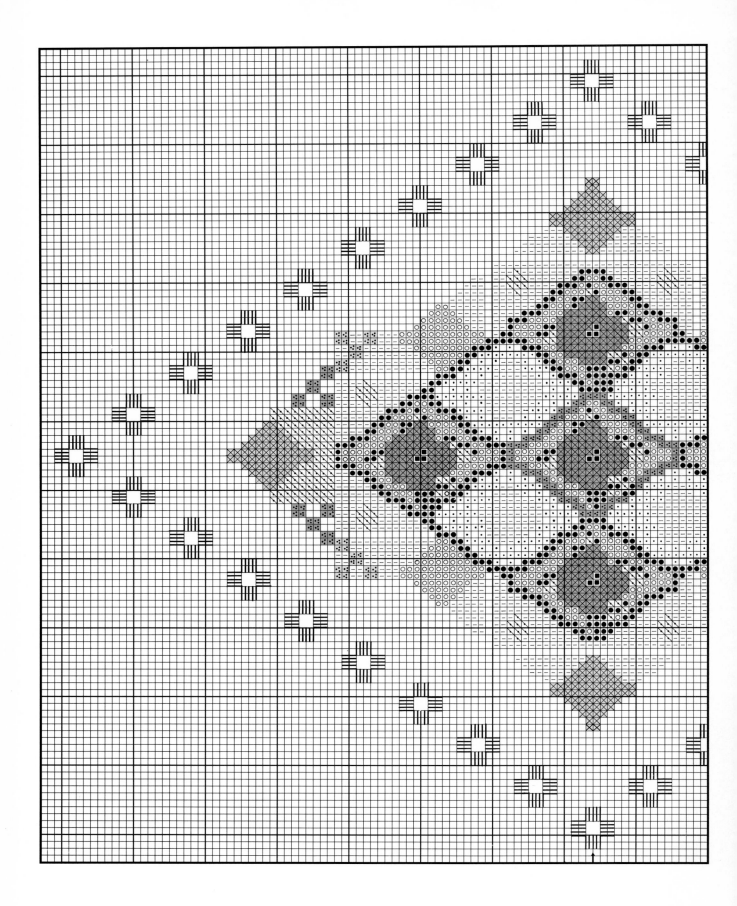

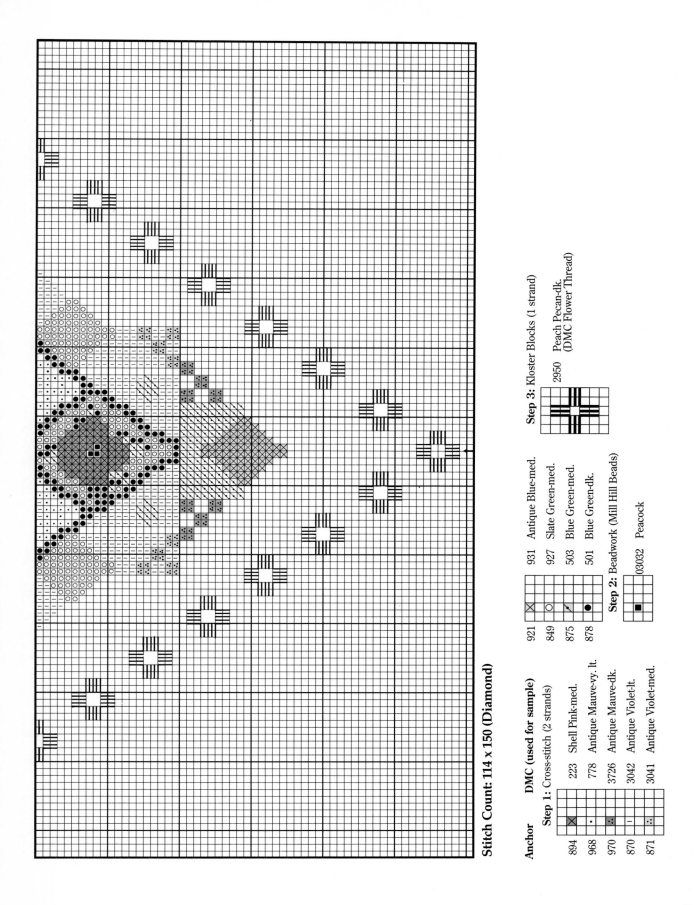

Stitch Count: 114 x 150 (Diamond)

Anchor	DMC (used for sample)
Step 1:	Cross-stitch (2 strands)
894	223 Shell Pink-med.
968	778 Antique Mauve-vy. lt.
970	3726 Antique Mauve-dk.
870	3042 Antique Violet-lt.
871	3041 Antique Violet-med.

921	Antique Blue-med.
849	927 Slate Green-med.
875	503 Blue Green-med.
878	501 Blue Green-dk.

Step 2: Beadwork (Mill Hill Beads)

03032	Peacock

Step 3: Kloster Blocks (1 strand)

2950	Peach Pecan-dk. (DMC Flower Thread)

45

Pleated Velvet Pillow

SAMPLE
Stitched on tea Linen 36 over 2 threads, the finished design size is 5⅜" x 3½" for 2 motifs. The fabric was cut 23" x 7". The graph contains 2 motifs. Choose 1 and begin stitching it in the center of the fabric. Then alternate the 2 motifs on each side of center for a total of 7 motifs.

FABRICS	DESIGN SIZES
Aida 11	8⅞" x 5⅝"
Aida 14	6⅞" x 4½"
Aida 18	5⅜" x 3½"
Hardanger 22	4⅜" x 2⅞"

MATERIALS
Completed cross-stitch on tea Linen 36
¾ yard of olive velveteen; matching thread
½ yard of muslin
1¼ yards (1½"-wide) flat trim
4 (3½") gold tassels
Polyester stuffing

DIRECTIONS
All seam allowances are ¼".

1. With design centered, trim design piece to 4" x 19½". From velveteen, cut 2 (5½" x 45") strips and 1 (14" x 19½") piece for pillow back. From muslin, cut 2 (14" x 19½") pieces.

2. Pin ¼"-deep pleats ½" apart across 1 long edge of velveteen strip (see Diagram). On other long edge of strip, make pleats in opposite direction, offsetting pleats as shown. Baste. The strip should measure 19½". Repeat for other strip.

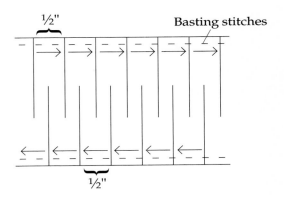

½"

Basting stitches

½"

Diagram

3. To make pillow front: With right sides facing and raw edges aligned, stitch 1 pleated velveteen strip to 1 long edge of design piece. Repeat with other strip along remaining edge of design piece.

4. Cut 2 (19½") lengths of trim. Slipstitch trim over seams on pillow front.

5. To line pillow front, layer design piece (right side up) on top of 1 muslin piece. Zigzag along all edges. Press as needed to keep layers flat. Repeat to line pillow back.

6. With right sides facing and raw edges aligned, stitch pillow front to back, leaving an opening for turning. Clip corners and turn. Stuff firmly. Slipstitch opening closed. Tack 1 tassel to each corner.

Stitch Count: 97 x 62 (for 2 motifs)

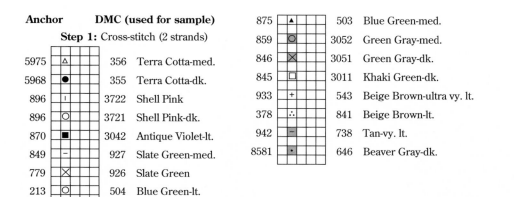

Anchor		DMC (used for sample)	
Step 1: Cross-stitch (2 strands)			
5975	△	356	Terra Cotta-med.
5968	●	355	Terra Cotta-dk.
896	ı	3722	Shell Pink
896	○	3721	Shell Pink-dk.
870	■	3042	Antique Violet-lt.
849	−	927	Slate Green-med.
779	✕	926	Slate Green
213	○	504	Blue Green-lt.

Anchor		DMC	
875	▲	503	Blue Green-med.
859	○	3052	Green Gray-med.
846	✕	3051	Green Gray-dk.
845	□	3011	Khaki Green-dk.
933	+	543	Beige Brown-ultra vy. lt.
378	∴	841	Beige Brown-lt.
942	−	738	Tan-vy. lt.
8581	·	646	Beaver Gray-dk.

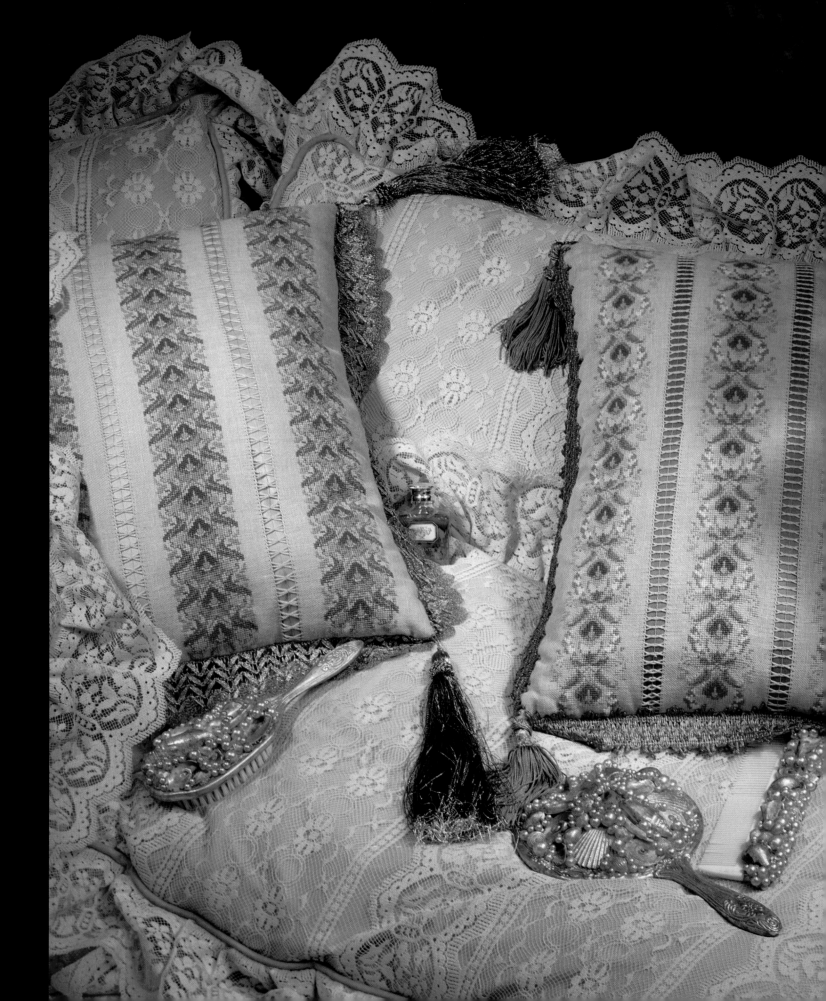

Hemstitched Pillows

SAMPLE for Floral Chain

Stitched on champagne Linen 28 over 2 threads, the finished design size is 2⅜" x 1¼" for 1 motif. The fabric was cut 17" x 23". Stitch 3 horizontal rows of 16 motifs each, leaving 2" of unworked linen between each row for hemstitching. Begin stitching 4¼" from 17" edge and 6¼" from 23" edge.

FABRICS	DESIGN SIZES
Aida 11	3" x 1½"
Aida 14	2⅜" x 1¼"
Aida 18	1⅞" x 1"
Hardanger 22	1½" x ¾"

SAMPLE for Leaf Chain

Stitched on champagne Linen 28 over 2 threads, the finished design size is 2⅜" x 2⅛" for 1 motif. The fabric was cut 17" x 23". Stitch 3 horizontal rows of 9 motifs each, leaving 2" of unworked linen between each row for hemstitching. Begin stitching 4¼" from 17" edge and 5½" from 23" edge.

FABRICS	DESIGN SIZES
Aida 11	3" x 2¾"
Aida 14	2⅜" x 2⅛"
Aida 18	1⅞" x 1⅝"
Hardanger 22	1½" x 1⅜"

MATERIALS (for 1 pillow)

Completed cross-stitch on moss green Linen 28
½ yard (45"-wide) lavender chintz fabric;
   matching thread
1¾ yards (2"-wide) flat antique gold trim
4 (4") gold tassels
Polyester stuffing

DIRECTIONS

All seam allowances are ¼".

1. With design centered, trim design piece to
13½" x 19½". Cut 2 (13½" x 19½") pieces of
lavender fabric (1 for lining and 1 for pillow
back).

2. To make lined pillow front, layer design piece
(right side up) on top of 1 piece of lavender fabric
(right side up). Zigzag along all edges. Press as
needed to keep layers flat.

3. With right sides facing and raw edges aligned,
stitch pillow front to pillow back, leaving an opening for turning. Clip corners and turn. Stuff firmly.
Slipstitch opening closed.

4. To attach trim, slipstitch 1 edge of trim to pillow
front along seams. Tack 1 tassel to each corner.

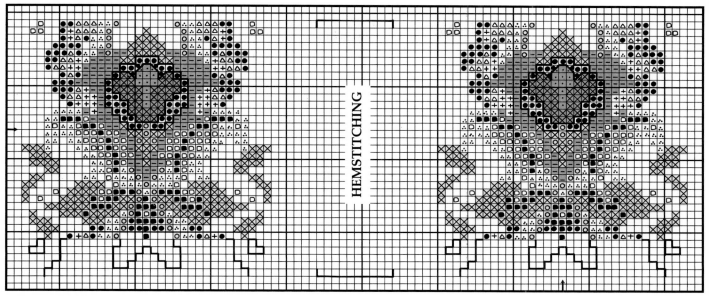

Floral Chain (Left Section)

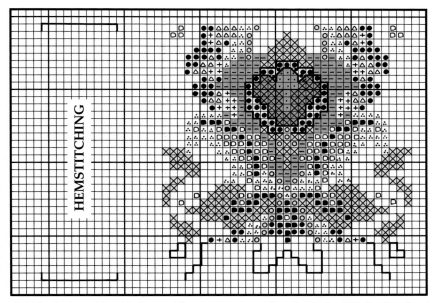

Stitch Count: 33 x 17 (1 motif)   **Floral Chain (Right Section)**

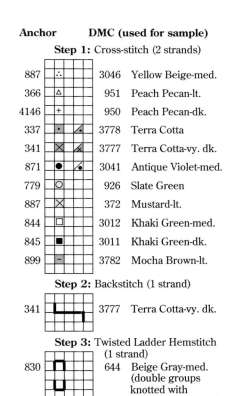

Anchor		DMC	(used for sample)

Step 1: Cross-stitch (2 strands)

887	∴		3046	Yellow Beige-med.
366	△		951	Peach Pecan-lt.
4146	+		950	Peach Pecan-dk.
337	⊡	◿	3778	Terra Cotta
341	⊠	◩	3777	Terra Cotta-vy. dk.
871	●	◓	3041	Antique Violet-med.
779	○		926	Slate Green
887	⊠		372	Mustard-lt.
844	☐		3012	Khaki Green-med.
845	■		3011	Khaki Green-dk.
899	–		3782	Mocha Brown-lt.

Step 2: Backstitch (1 strand)

341		3777	Terra Cotta-vy. dk.

Step 3: Twisted Ladder Hemstitch (1 strand)

830		644	Beige Gray-med. (double groups knotted with vertical thread)

Anchor **DMC** (used for sample)

Step 1: Cross-stitch (2 strands)

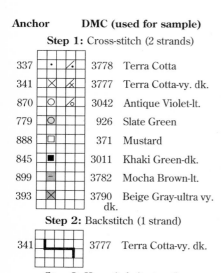

337	3778	Terra Cotta
341	3777	Terra Cotta-vy. dk.
870	3042	Antique Violet-lt.
779	926	Slate Green
888	371	Mustard
845	3011	Khaki Green-dk.
899	3782	Mocha Brown-lt.
393	3790	Beige Gray-ultra vy. dk.

Step 2: Backstitch (1 strand)

| 341 | 3777 | Terra Cotta-vy. dk. |

Step 3: Hemstitch (1 strand)

| 830 | 644 | Beige Gray-med. (triple groups knotted with vertical thread) |

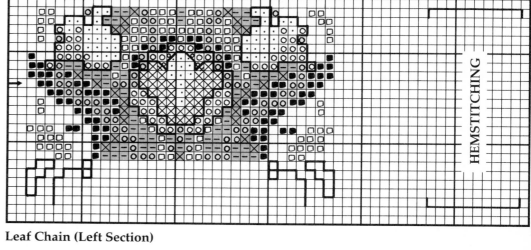

HEMSTITCHING

Leaf Chain (Left Section)

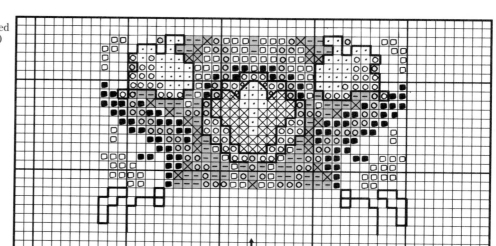

Leaf Chain (Middle Section)

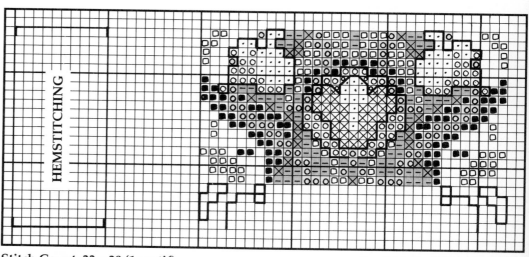

HEMSTITCHING

Stitch Count: 33 x 30 (1 motif)

Leaf Chain (Right Section)

54

Butterfly Pillow

SAMPLE

Stitched on driftwood Belfast Linen 32 over 2 threads, the finished design size is 2½" x 5⅝". The fabric was cut 16" x 7".

FABRICS	DESIGN SIZES
Aida 11	3⅝" x 8⅛"
Aida 14	2⅞" x 6⅜"
Aida 18	2¼" x 5"
Hardanger 22	1⅞" x 4⅛"

MATERIALS

Completed cross-stitch on driftwood Belfast Linen 32; matching thread
¼ yard of unstitched driftwood Belfast Linen 32
1 (12½" x 3¼") piece of flannel
¾ yard (½"-wide) lace trim
¾ yard (⅛"-wide) peach ribbon
Polyester stuffing

DIRECTIONS

All seam allowances are ¼".

1. With design centered, trim design piece to 12½" x 3¼". From unstitched linen, cut 1 (12½" x 3¼") strip and 2 (9½" x 9") pieces.

2. Cut 2 (12½") lengths each of lace trim and ribbon. Weave 1 length of ribbon through each length of lace trim (see photo); set aside.

3. To make pillow band, layer design piece (right side up) on top of flannel. Zigzag along all edges. With right sides facing and raw edges aligned, stitch 1 length of lace to each long edge of design piece. With right sides facing and raw edges aligned, stitch design piece and unstitched linen strip together along long edges. Turn.

4. To finish band, fold band in half widthwise with right sides facing and stitch ends of band together. Press seam open. Topstitch across ends so that seam allowance is flat.

5. To make pillow, with right sides facing and raw edges aligned, stitch 9½" x 9" linen pieces together, leaving an opening for turning. Clip corners and turn. Stuff moderately. Slipstitch opening closed.

6. Slide pillow band around middle of pillow, easing fullness (see photo).

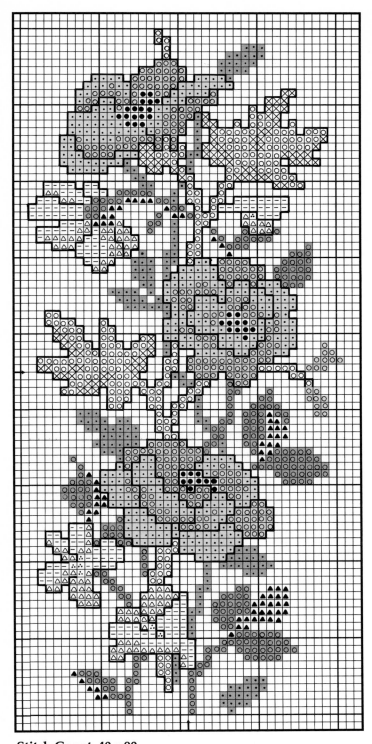

Stitch Count: 40 x 90

Anchor		DMC (used for sample)	
		Step 1: Cross-stitch (2 strands)	
300	∴	745	Yellow-lt. pale
778	·	948	Peach-vy. lt.
8	◎	353	Peach
25	–	3326	Rose-lt.
66	△	3688	Mauve-med.
10	●	352	Coral-lt.
213	▪	504	Blue Green-lt.
214	⊙	368	Pistachio Green-lt.
216	▲	367	Pistachio Green-dk.
265	○	3348	Yellow Green-lt.
266	✕	3347	Yellow Green-med.
		Step 2: Backstitch (1 strand)	
69		3687	Mauve (flowers)
257		3346	Hunter Green (leaves, stems)

Royal Rose Pillow

SAMPLE
Stitched on black Dublin Linen 25 over 2 threads, the finished design size is 9½" x 7½" for 1 motif. The fabric was cut 18" x 18". Center large rose from inner band 2" above fabric center and begin stitching (bold lines on graph indicate placement for repeat).

FABRICS	DESIGN SIZES
Aida 11	10⅞" x 8½"
Aida 14	8½" x 6⅝"
Aida 18	6⅝" x 5⅛"
Hardanger 22	5⅜" x 4¼"

MATERIALS
Completed cross-stitch on black Dublin Linen 25; matching thread
1 (16"-square) piece of unstitched black Dublin Linen 25
1½ yards (45"-wide) red velvet
½ yard of black fusible interfacing
2 yards (⅜"-wide) red/gold braid trim
Polyester stuffing

DIRECTIONS
All seam allowances are ¼".

1. With design centered, trim design piece to 16" square. From red velvet, cut 6 (8" x 44") strips. Following manufacturer's instructions, fuse interfacing to wrong side of design piece and unstitched black linen.

2. Stitch red velvet strips end to end to make 1 long strip. Pin pleats ½" deep and ½" apart on both long edges until you have 14" of pleated velvet; baste. Steam-press for crushed velvet effect. Then make 3" of pleated velvet with ½"-deep pleats ¼" apart to allow extra fullness at corner. Repeat 3 times, alternating 14" lengths of pleated velvet with 3" lengths of pleated velvet, for a total of 4 of each length.

3. With right sides facing and raw edges aligned, center 3" lengths of pleated velvet on corners of design piece, easing 14" lengths of pleated velvet to fit straight edges; stitch. Repeat with unstitched black linen, leaving an opening for turning. Turn and stuff. Slipstitch opening closed.

4. Slipstitch red/gold trim to seam around design piece.

Stitch Count: 119 x 93 (1 motif)

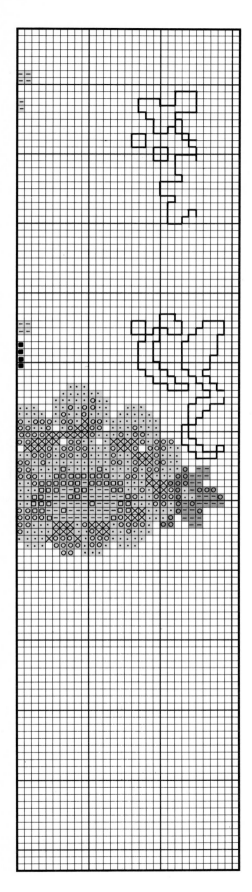

DMC   **Medicis (used for sample)**

Step 1: Cross-stitch (1 strand of Medicis or 2 strands of DMC)

DMC		Medicis	
350	▲	8128	Coral-med.
321	•	8130	Christmas Red
304	○	8102	Christmas Red-med.
814	⊠	8100	Garnet-dk.
223	–	8107	Shell Pink-med.
221	▢	8106	Shell Pink-vy. dk.
554	▬	8896	Violet-lt.
553	◯	8895	Violet-med.
3726	∴	8122	Antique Mauve-dk.
470	▪	8412	Avocado Green-lt.
730	⊠	8422	Olive Green-vy. dk.
368	▢	8406	Pistachio Green-lt.
367	■	8414	Pistachio Green-dk.

Beaded Monogrammed Pillow

SAMPLE

Stitched on cream Belfast Linen 32 over 2 threads, the finished design size is 6¾" x 5¼". The fabric was cut 14" x 12". Because of the bead size, the design is suitable only for 14 - and 16-count fabrics. See Suppliers for Mill Hill Beads.

FABRICS	DESIGN SIZES
Aida 14	7⅝" x 6"
Aida 16	6¾" x 5¼"

MATERIALS

Completed design on cream Belfast Linen 32; matching thread
¼ yard of unstitched cream Belfast Linen 32
15 (250-count) packages of #03005 Platinum Rose Mill Hill Beads
Polyester stuffing
Beading needle

DIRECTIONS

All seam allowances are ¼".

1. With design centered, trim design piece to 8" x 9¾" for pillow front. Cut unstitched linen to match design piece.

2. With right sides facing and raw edges aligned, stitch design piece to unstitched linen, leaving an opening for turning. Trim corners and turn. Stuff firmly. Slipstitch opening closed.

3. Thread beading needle, securing thread at 1 corner seam. Place 5 beads on thread and stitch ¼"-long diagonal whipstitch over seam. Continue to make stitches approximately ⅛" apart with 5 beads on thread around pillow (see Diagram A). Secure thread.

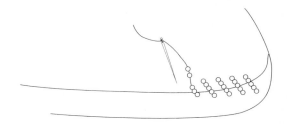

Diagram A

4. To make bead loops, secure thread at 1 corner. Place 40 beads on thread and, skipping 1 whipstitch, stitch through seam from bottom to top (see Diagram B). Bring next loop of beads behind first and skip 1 whipstitch; continue stitching through seam from bottom to top. Continue around pillow.

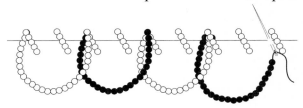

Diagram B

Mill Hill Beads

(used for sample)

Step 1: Beadwork (Mill Hill Beads)

O	03005 Platinum Rose
X	03023 Platinum Violet

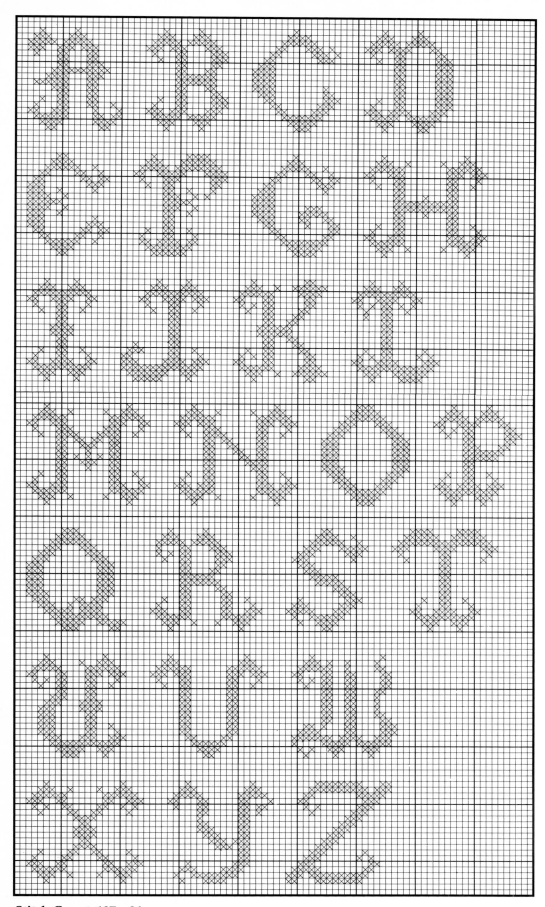

Stitch Count: 107 x 84

Quatrefoil Medallion Pillow

SAMPLE
Stitched on gray Glenshee Linen 29 over 2 threads, the finished design size is 13" x 13". The fabric was cut 19" x 19". Begin stitching bottom of design 1" above fabric center (bold lines on graph indicate placement for repeat).

FABRICS	DESIGN SIZES
Aida 11	13¾" x 13¾"
Aida 14	10¾" x 10¾"
Aida 18	8⅜" x 8⅜"
Hardanger 22	6⅞" x 6⅞"

MATERIALS
Completed cross-stitch on gray Glenshee Linen 29;
  matching thread
¼ yard (54"-wide) mauve upholstery fabric;
  matching thread
½ yard of gray velveteen
1⅓ yards (½") gray flat braid
1½ yards (½") light pink satin cording
4 (3") light pink tassels
1 (16½"-square) piece of muslin
Dressmaker's pen
Polyester stuffing

DIRECTIONS
All seam allowances are ¼".

1. With design centered, trim design piece to 16" square. From upholstery fabric, cut 4 (12" x 8") pieces. From velveteen, cut 1 (16½"-square) piece.

2. Place design piece (right side up) diagonally over muslin, matching corners of design to centers of each edge of muslin. Baste.

3. To make pillow corners, mark center of each 12" edge on right side of upholstery fabric, using dressmaker's pen; draw a line between marks. With right sides facing, fold 1 piece in half widthwise to measure 6" x 8" and stitch along 1 (6") end.

Unfold fabric piece. With right sides facing and raw edges aligned, stitch other 12" edge to 1 corner of design piece, 1" outside design area. Repeat for remaining 3 corners.

With raw edges aligned, zigzag raw edges of corner pieces and muslin together.

4. To gather corners, use a double strand of thread and run a gathering stitch by hand from top of 6" seam of corner piece along marked line to edge of design piece (see Diagram A). Pull to gather so that corner of seam meets edge of design piece and forms folds in corner fabric (see Diagram B). Tuck corner under folds. Secure thread. Repeat for remaining 3 corners.

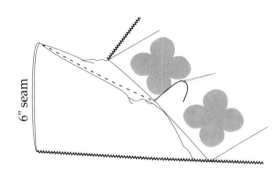

6" seam

Diagram A

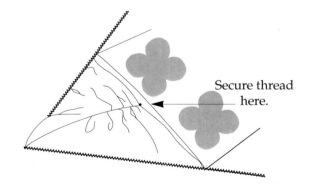

Secure thread here.

Diagram B

5. With right sides facing and raw edges aligned, stitch pillow front to pillow back, leaving an opening in center of 1 edge for turning. Turn.

6. Slipstitch braid to design piece just inside seam. Beginning at corner of design piece at opening, tack pink cording over seam, tying a knot in cording at each corner (see Diagram C). Tuck ends of cording in opening. Stuff firmly. Slipstitch opening closed. Tack 1 tassel securely to each corner.

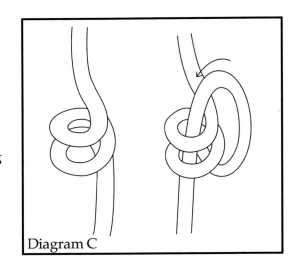

Diagram C

Anchor		DMC (used for sample)	
	Step 1: Cross-stitch (2 strands)		
886	–	3047	Yellow Beige-lt.
892	∴	225	Shell Pink-vy. lt.
893	⊠	224	Shell Pink-lt.
894	○	223	Shell Pink-med.
969	◍	316	Antique Mauve-med.
970	●	315	Antique Mauve-vy. dk.
846	⊠	3051	Green Gray-dk.

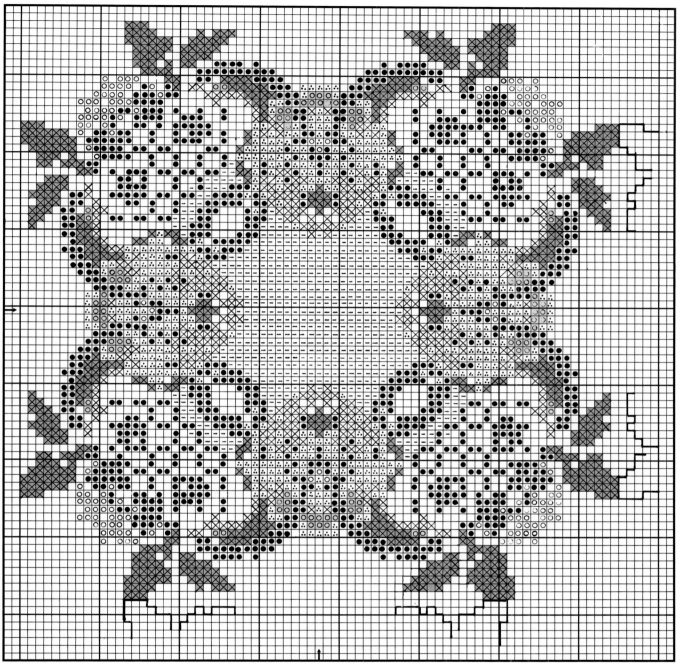

Stitch Count: 150 x 150

Framing Spring's Art

*T*houghts of springtime
bring so many wonderful pleasures
to mind—beautiful flowers in an
array of exquisite colors, birds
singing in blossoming trees, and the
laughter of children at play after
a long, cold winter. Enjoy a
refreshing touch of spring all year
long with these fanciful
framed pieces.

Wood Nymphs

SAMPLE
Stitched on cream Belfast Linen 32 over 2 threads, the finished design size is 7¾" x 11½". The fabric was cut 14" x 18".

FABRICS	DESIGN SIZES
Aida 11	10⅞" x 16⅛"
Aida 14	8⅝" x 12¾"
Aida 18	6⅝" x 9⅞"
Hardanger 22	5½" x 8⅛"

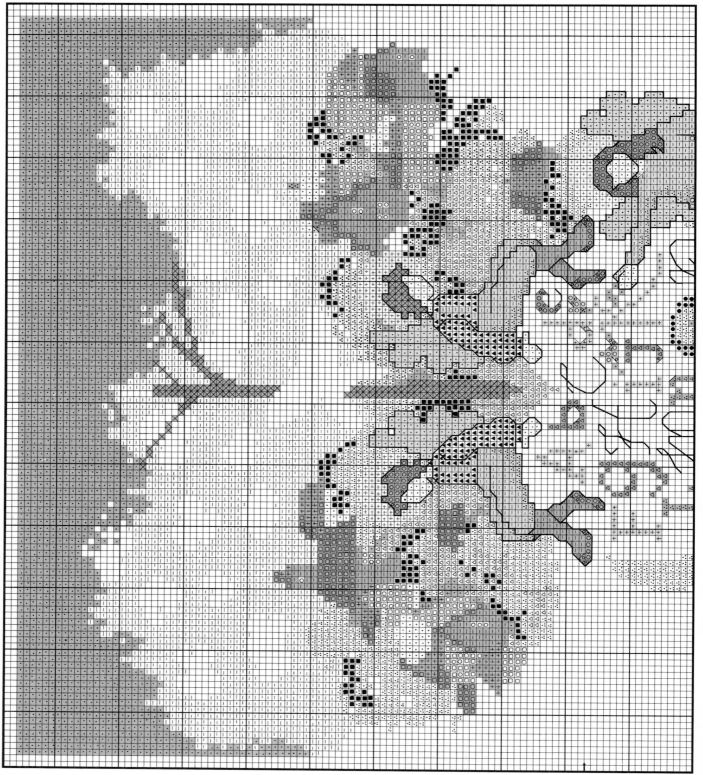

Stitch Count: 120 x 178

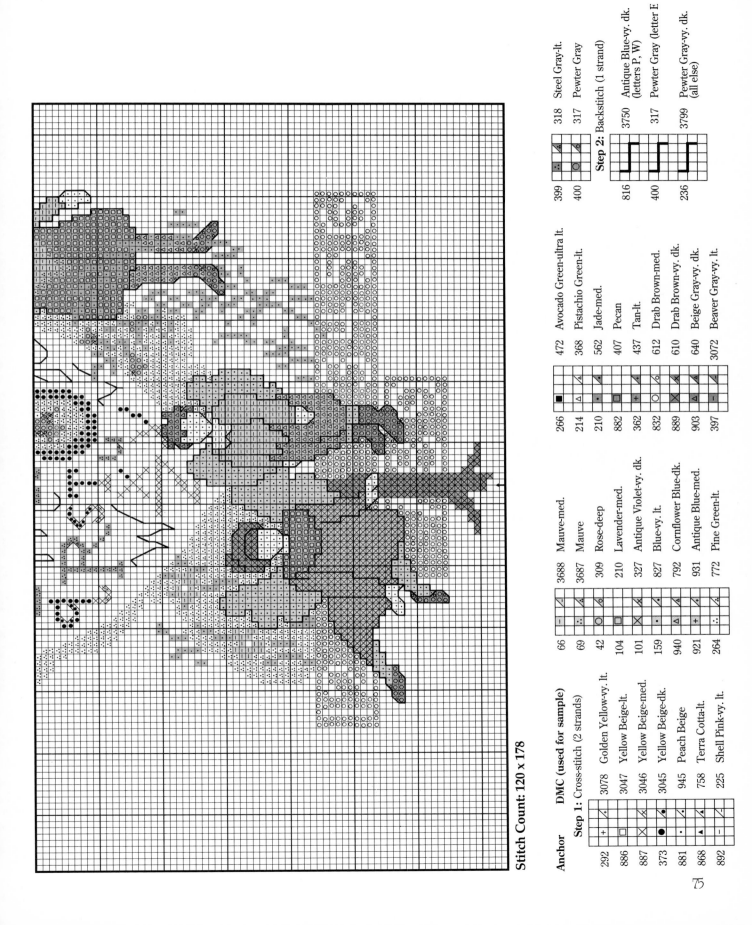

Anchor		DMC (used for sample)	

Step 1: Cross-stitch (2 strands)

Anchor	DMC	Color
292	3078	Golden Yellow-vy. lt.
886	3047	Yellow Beige-lt.
887	3046	Yellow Beige-med.
373	3045	Yellow Beige-dk.
881	945	Peach Beige
868	758	Terra Cotta-lt.
892	225	Shell Pink-vy. lt.
66	3688	Mauve-med.
69	3687	Mauve
42	309	Rose-deep
104	210	Lavender-med.
101	327	Antique Violet-vy. dk.
159	827	Blue-vy. lt.
940	792	Cornflower Blue-dk.
921	931	Antique Blue-med.
264	772	Pine Green-lt.
266	472	Avocado Green-ultra lt.
214	368	Pistachio Green-lt.
210	562	Jade-med.
882	407	Pecan
362	437	Tan-lt.
832	612	Drab Brown-med.
889	610	Drab Brown-vy. dk.
903	640	Beige Gray-vy. dk.
397	3072	Beaver Gray-vy. lt.
399	318	Steel Gray-lt.
400	317	Pewter Gray

Step 2: Backstitch (1 strand)

Anchor	DMC	Color
816	3750	Antique Blue-vy. dk. (letters P, W)
400	317	Pewter Gray (letter E)
236	3799	Pewter Gray-vy. dk. (all else)

Splendid Blossoms

SAMPLE
Stitched on antique green Linen 28 over 2 threads,
the finished design size is 8⅜" x 9¼". The fabric
was cut 15" x 16".

FABRICS	DESIGN SIZES
Aida 11	10¾" x 11⅞"
Aida 14	8⅜" x 9¼"
Aida 18	6½" x 7¼"
Hardanger 22	5⅜" x 5⅞"

(Top Section)

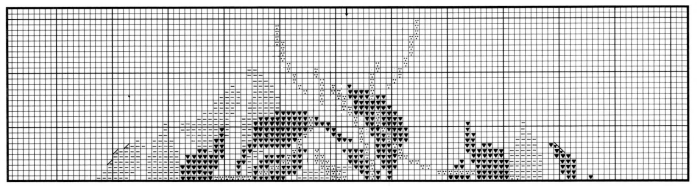

Stitch Count: 118 x 130

(Bottom Section)

Anchor		DMC (used for sample)

Step 1: Cross-stitch (2 strands)

Anchor		DMC	
969	▪	3726	Antique Mauve-dk.
970	◉	315	Antique Mauve-vy. dk.
871	▪	3041	Antique Violet-med.
872	○	3740	Antique Violet-dk.
840	□	3768	Slate Green-dk.
876	– ╱	502	Blue Green
878	△	501	Blue Green-dk.
879	▲ ╱	500	Blue Green-vy. dk.
379	∴	840	Beige Brown-med.

Be Mine

SAMPLE

Stitched on English rose Linen 28 over 2 threads, the finished design size is 8⅝" x 6". The fabric was cut 15" x 12".

FABRICS	DESIGN SIZES
Aida 11	10⅞" x 7⅝"
Aida 14	8⅝" x 6"
Aida 18	6⅝" x 4⅝"
Hardanger 22	5½" x 3⅞"

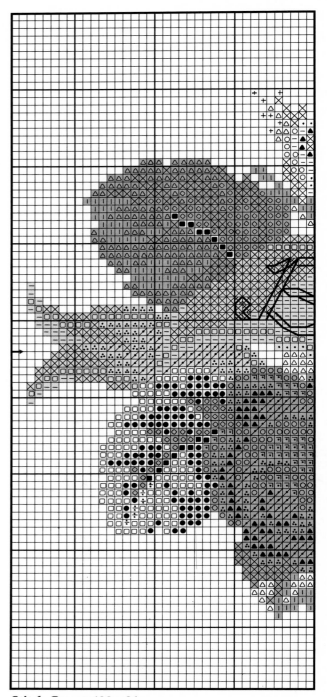

Stitch Count: 120 x 84

Anchor		DMC (used for sample)	

Step 1: Cross-stitch (2 strands)

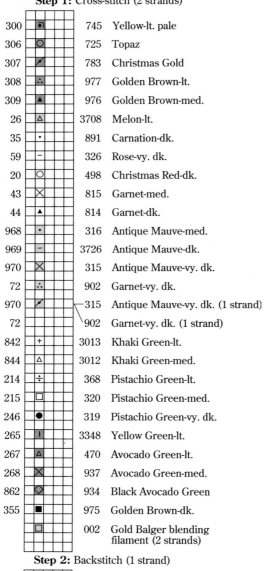

300	745	Yellow-lt. pale
306	725	Topaz
307	783	Christmas Gold
308	977	Golden Brown-lt.
309	976	Golden Brown-med.
26	3708	Melon-lt.
35	891	Carnation-dk.
59	326	Rose-vy. dk.
20	498	Christmas Red-dk.
43	815	Garnet-med.
44	814	Garnet-dk.
968	316	Antique Mauve-med.
969	3726	Antique Mauve-dk.
970	315	Antique Mauve-vy. dk.
72	902	Garnet-vy. dk.
970	315	Antique Mauve-vy. dk. (1 strand)
72	902	Garnet-vy. dk. (1 strand)
842	3013	Khaki Green-lt.
844	3012	Khaki Green-med.
214	368	Pistachio Green-lt.
215	320	Pistachio Green-med.
246	319	Pistachio Green-vy. dk.
265	3348	Yellow Green-lt.
267	470	Avocado Green-lt.
268	937	Avocado Green-med.
862	934	Black Avocado Green
355	975	Golden Brown-dk.
	002	Gold Balger blending filament (2 strands)

Step 2: Backstitch (1 strand)

| 862 | 934 | Black Avocado Green |

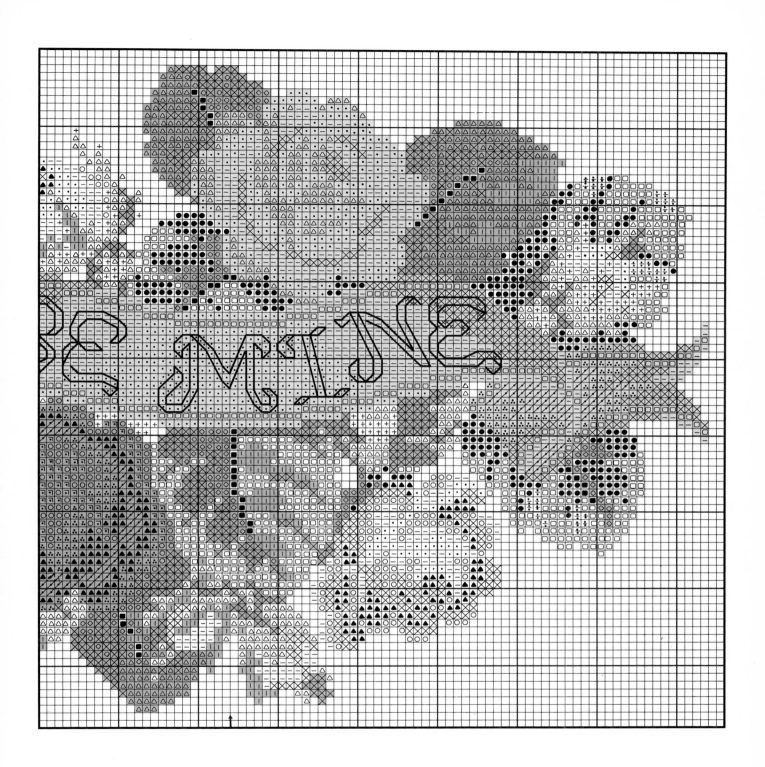

Trellis Roses

SAMPLE
Stitched on white Belfast Linen 32 over 2 threads, the finished design size is 8¾" x 12⅛". The fabric was cut 15" x 19".

FABRICS	DESIGN SIZES
Aida 11	12⅞" x 17⅝"
Aida 14	10⅛" x 13⅞"
Aida 18	7⅞" x 10¾"
Hardanger 22	6⅜" x 8⅞"

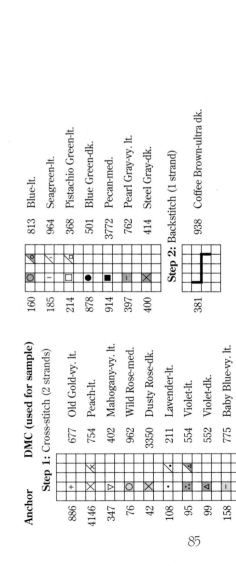

Stitch Count: 141 x 194

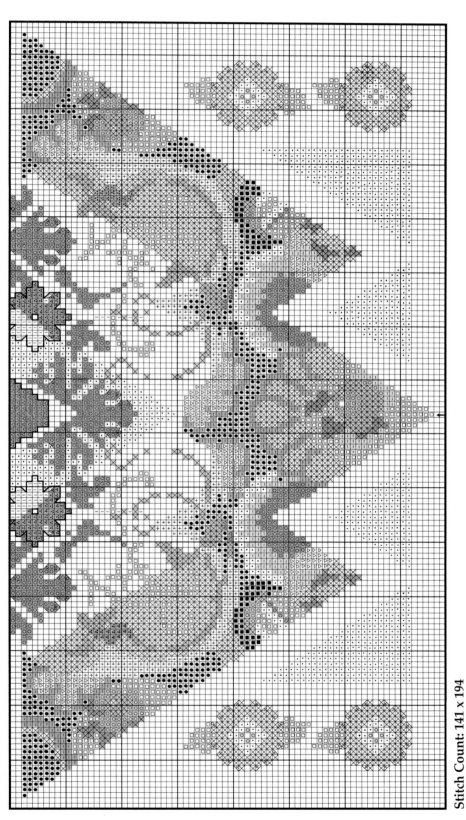

Anchor		DMC (used for sample)

Step 1: Cross-stitch (2 strands)

886	+	677	Old Gold-vy. lt.
4146	⊠	754	Peach-lt.
347	▷	402	Mahogany-vy. lt.
76	⊙	962	Wild Rose-med.
42	✕	3350	Dusty Rose-dk.
108	·	211	Lavender-lt.
95	⋮	554	Violet-lt.
99	◁	552	Violet-dk.
158	—	775	Baby Blue-vy. lt.
160	⊙	813	Blue-lt.
185	–	964	Seagreen-lt.
214	▱	368	Pistachio Green-lt.
878	●	501	Blue Green-dk.
914	■	3772	Pecan-med.
397	▮	762	Pearl Gray-vy. lt.
400	⊠	414	Steel Gray-dk.

Step 2: Backstitch (1 strand)

381		938	Coffee Brown-ultra dk.

The Garden Party

SAMPLE

Stitched on cream Belfast Linen 32 over 2 threads, the finished design size is 9⅞" x 13⅜". The fabric was cut 16" x 20".

FABRICS	DESIGN SIZES
Aida 11	13¹⁵⁄₁₆" x 19¹⁵⁄₁₆"
Aida 14	10¹⁵⁄₁₆" x 15⅝"
Aida 18	8½" x 12⅛"
Hardanger 22	7¼" x 10"

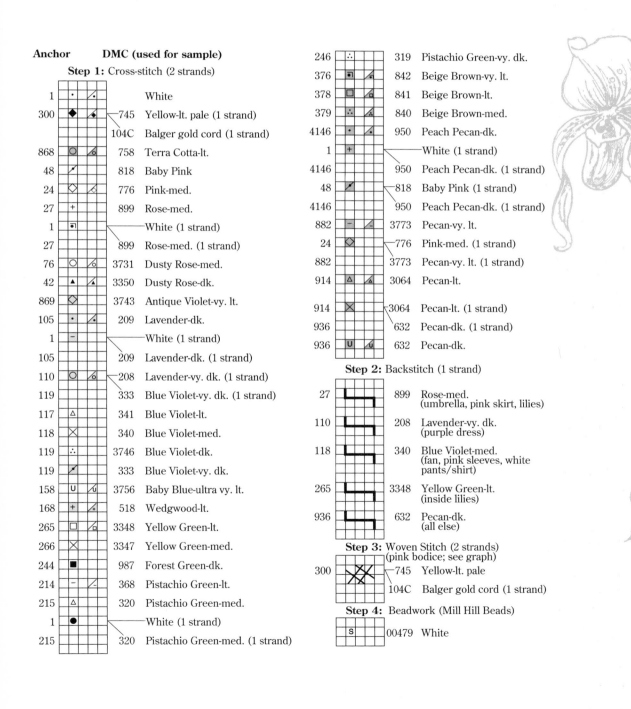

Anchor   DMC (used for sample)

Step 1: Cross-stitch (2 strands)

1	White
300	745 Yellow-lt. pale (1 strand)
	104C Balger gold cord (1 strand)
868	758 Terra Cotta-lt.
48	818 Baby Pink
24	776 Pink-med.
27	899 Rose-med.
1	White (1 strand)
27	899 Rose-med. (1 strand)
76	3731 Dusty Rose-med.
42	3350 Dusty Rose-dk.
869	3743 Antique Violet-vy. lt.
105	209 Lavender-dk.
1	White (1 strand)
105	209 Lavender-dk. (1 strand)
110	208 Lavender-vy. dk. (1 strand)
119	333 Blue Violet-vy. dk. (1 strand)
117	341 Blue Violet-lt.
118	340 Blue Violet-med.
119	3746 Blue Violet-dk.
119	333 Blue Violet-vy. dk.
158	3756 Baby Blue-ultra vy. lt.
168	518 Wedgwood-lt.
265	3348 Yellow Green-lt.
266	3347 Yellow Green-med.
244	987 Forest Green-dk.
214	368 Pistachio Green-lt.
215	320 Pistachio Green-med.
1	White (1 strand)
215	320 Pistachio Green-med. (1 strand)

246	319 Pistachio Green-vy. dk.
376	842 Beige Brown-vy. lt.
378	841 Beige Brown-lt.
379	840 Beige Brown-med.
4146	950 Peach Pecan-dk.
1	White (1 strand)
4146	950 Peach Pecan-dk. (1 strand)
48	818 Baby Pink (1 strand)
4146	950 Peach Pecan-dk. (1 strand)
882	3773 Pecan-vy. lt.
24	776 Pink-med. (1 strand)
882	3773 Pecan-vy. lt. (1 strand)
914	3064 Pecan-lt.
914	3064 Pecan-lt. (1 strand)
936	632 Pecan-dk. (1 strand)
936	632 Pecan-dk.

Step 2: Backstitch (1 strand)

27	899 Rose-med. (umbrella, pink skirt, lilies)
110	208 Lavender-vy. dk. (purple dress)
118	340 Blue Violet-med. (fan, pink sleeves, white pants/shirt)
265	3348 Yellow Green-lt. (inside lilies)
936	632 Pecan-dk. (all else)

Step 3: Woven Stitch (2 strands) (pink bodice; see graph)

300	745 Yellow-lt. pale
	104C Balger gold cord (1 strand)

Step 4: Beadwork (Mill Hill Beads)

	00479 White

(Top Section)

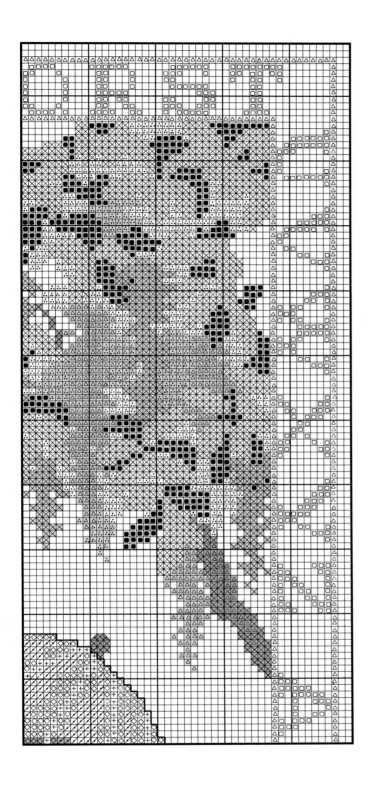

Stitch Count: 153 x 219

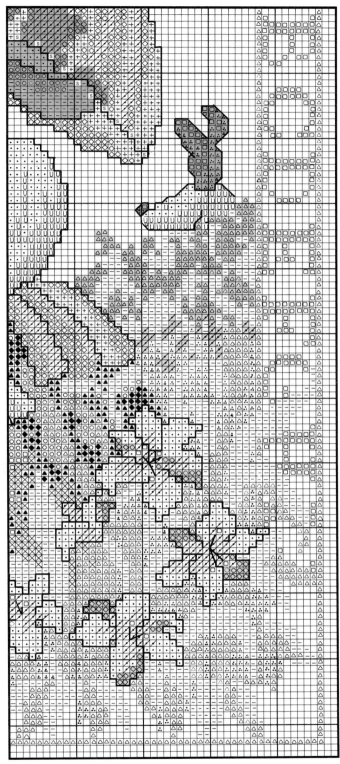

(Bottom Section)

Summer's Hummers

SAMPLE

Stitched on shell Linen 28 over 2 threads, the finished design size is 5⅞" x 7⅜". The fabric was cut 12" x 14". The completed design was placed in an antique oval frame.

FABRICS	DESIGN SIZES
Aida 11	7½" x 9⅜"
Aida 14	5⅞" x 7⅜"
Aida 18	6½" x 5¾"
Hardanger 22	3¾" x 4⅝"

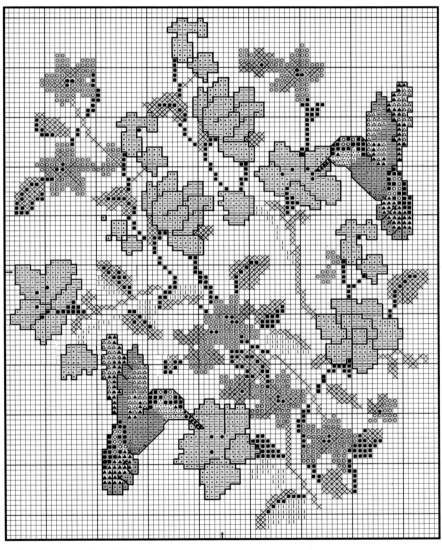

Stitch Count: 82 x 103

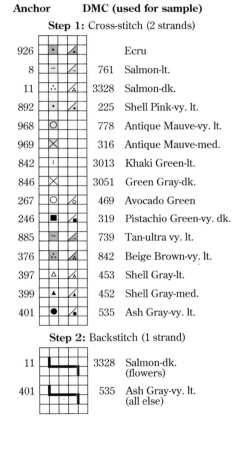

Anchor			DMC	(used for sample)
		Step 1: Cross-stitch (2 strands)		
926				Ecru
8			761	Salmon-lt.
11			3328	Salmon-dk.
892			225	Shell Pink-vy. lt.
968			778	Antique Mauve-vy. lt.
969			316	Antique Mauve-med.
842			3013	Khaki Green-lt.
846			3051	Green Gray-dk.
267			469	Avocado Green
246			319	Pistachio Green-vy. dk.
885			739	Tan-ultra vy. lt.
376			842	Beige Brown-vy. lt.
397			453	Shell Gray-lt.
399			452	Shell Gray-med.
401			535	Ash Gray-vy. lt.
		Step 2: Backstitch (1 strand)		
11			3328	Salmon-dk. (flowers)
401			535	Ash Gray-vy. lt. (all else)

Arbor Pastels

SAMPLE
Stitched on pink Damask Aida 18 over 1 thread, the finished design size is 5⅜" x 7⅜". The fabric was cut 12" x 14".

FABRICS	DESIGN SIZES
Aida 11	8⅞" x 11⅞"
Aida 14	6⅞" x 9⅜"
Hardanger 22	4⅜" x 6"

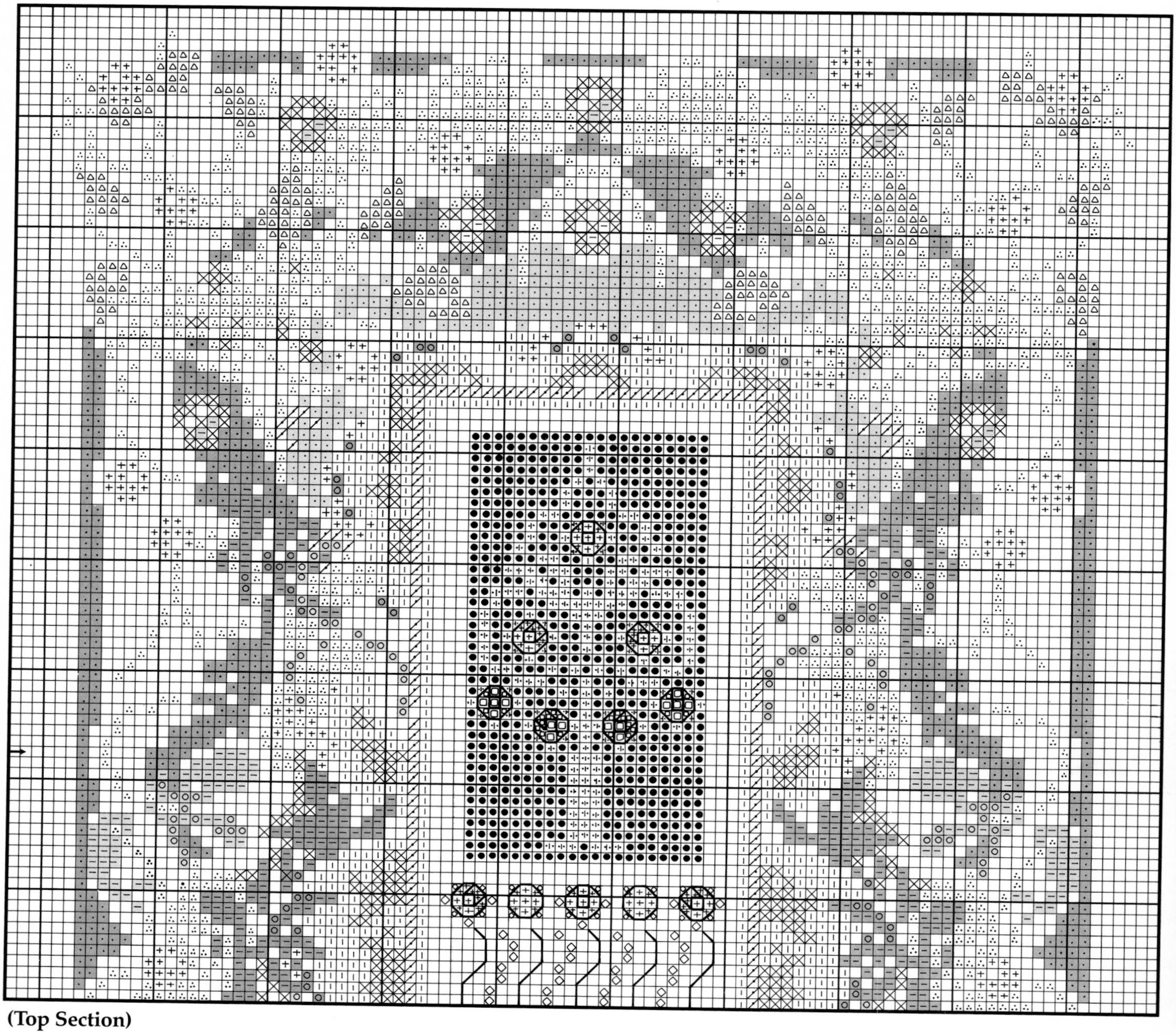

(Top Section)

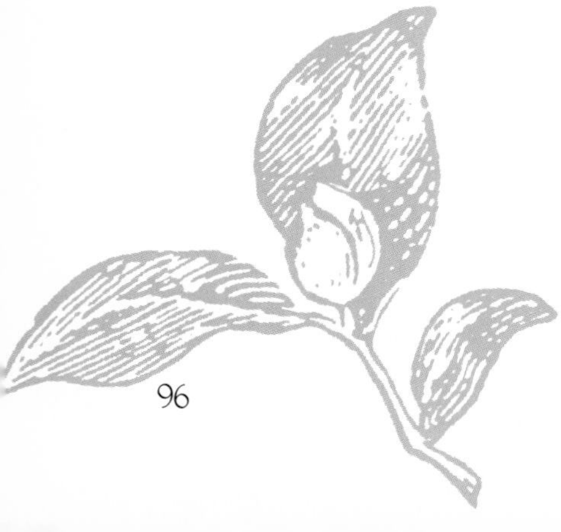

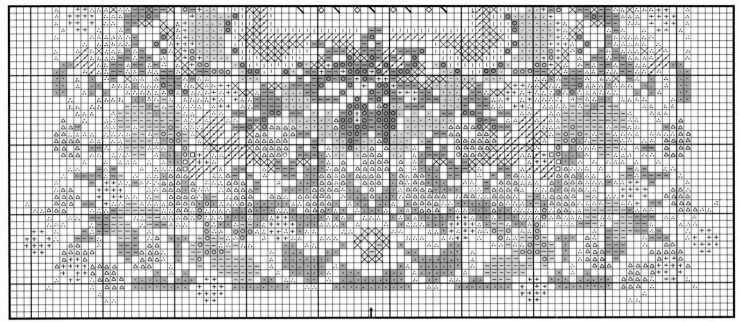

Stitch Count: 97 x 131

(Bottom Section)

Anchor | **DMC** (used for sample)

Step 1: Cross-stitch (2 strands)

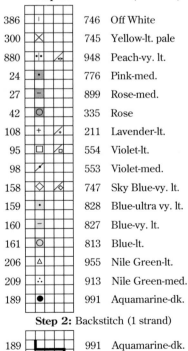

386	746	Off White
300	745	Yellow-lt. pale
880	948	Peach-vy. lt.
24	776	Pink-med.
27	899	Rose-med.
42	335	Rose
108	211	Lavender-lt.
95	554	Violet-lt.
98	553	Violet-med.
158	747	Sky Blue-vy. lt.
159	828	Blue-ultra vy. lt.
160	827	Blue-vy. lt.
161	813	Blue-lt.
206	955	Nile Green-lt.
209	913	Nile Green-med.
189	991	Aquamarine-dk.

Step 2: Backstitch (1 strand)

| 189 | 991 | Aquamarine-dk. |

The Goose Girl

SAMPLE
Stitched on light blue Aida 14 over 1 thread, the finished design size for the background is 6½" x 4¼". Stitched on Silk Gauze 30 over 2 threads, the finished design size for the foreground is 6⅜" x 4⅛". The fabric was cut 13" x 11" for each.

To create a 3-dimensional effect, place a ¼" spacer between the background piece and the foreground piece when framing, centering the foreground piece on top of the background piece and aligning the bottom edges of the design.

Stitch Count: 95 x 62 (Foreground)

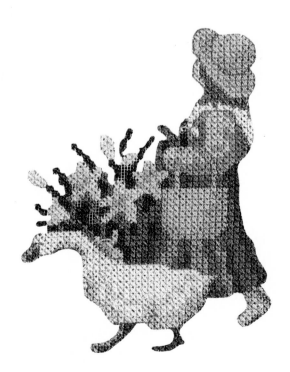

Stitch Count: 91 x 59 (Background)

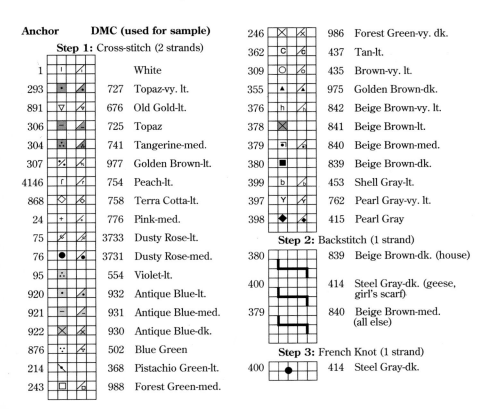

Anchor			DMC	(used for sample)
Step 1: Cross-stitch (2 strands)				
1	I	/		White
293	•	◢	727	Topaz-vy. lt.
891	▽	◿	676	Old Gold-lt.
306	▬	◢	725	Topaz
304	∴	◢	741	Tangerine-med.
307	◿	◿	977	Golden Brown-lt.
4146	Γ	/	754	Peach-lt.
868	◇	◈	758	Terra Cotta-lt.
24	+	◢	776	Pink-med.
75	◿	◢	3733	Dusty Rose-lt.
76	●	◖	3731	Dusty Rose-med.
95	∴		554	Violet-lt.
920	•	◢	932	Antique Blue-lt.
921	▬	◢	931	Antique Blue-med.
922	☒	◢	930	Antique Blue-dk.
876	∷	◢	502	Blue Green
214	◥	◢	368	Pistachio Green-lt.
243	☐	◿	988	Forest Green-med.
246	☒	◹	986	Forest Green-vy. dk.
362	C	◿	437	Tan-lt.
309	O	◢	435	Brown-vy. lt.
355	▲	◢	975	Golden Brown-dk.
376	h	◢	842	Beige Brown-vy. lt.
378	☒		841	Beige Brown-lt.
379	◙	◢	840	Beige Brown-med.
380	■		839	Beige Brown-dk.
399	b	◢	453	Shell Gray-lt.
397	Y	◢	762	Pearl Gray-vy. lt.
398	◆	◢	415	Pearl Gray

Step 2: Backstitch (1 strand)

380		839	Beige Brown-dk. (house)
400		414	Steel Gray-dk. (geese, girl's scarf)
379		840	Beige Brown-med. (all else)

Step 3: French Knot (1 strand)

400	●	414	Steel Gray-dk.

Tokens of Affection

*O*bjects made by a
loving hand needn't be grand
or costly. Fashion delicate
keepsakes filled with sweet
scents or embellish a gift for a
sentimental touch. Each of
these endearing treasures
expresses fondness of the heart,
bringing joy to both creator
and recipient.

Heavenly Scents

SAMPLE for Pink Sachet
Stitched on a purchased 18"-square natural linen handkerchief using Waste Canvas 14 over 1 thread, the finished design size is 2¾" x 2¾". The canvas was cut 5" x 5". Center and baste the canvas at a 45° angle on 1 corner of the handkerchief. Begin stitching 2½" from the corner and 1¼" from the edges of the handkerchief.

FABRICS	DESIGN SIZES
Aida 11	3½" x 3½"
Aida 14	2¾" x 2¾"
Aida 18	2⅛" x 2⅛"
Hardanger 22	1¾" x 1¾"

SAMPLE for Dark Green Sachet
Stitched on a purchased 18"-square natural linen handkerchief using Waste Canvas 14 over 1 thread, the finished design size is 2¾" x 2¾". The canvas was cut 5" x 5". Center and baste the canvas at a 45° angle on 1 corner of the handkerchief. Begin stitching 2½" from the corner and 1¼" from the edges of the handkerchief.

FABRICS	DESIGN SIZES
Aida 11	3½" x 3½"
Aida 14	2¾" x 2¾"
Aida 18	2⅛" x 2⅛"
Hardanger 22	1¾" x 1¾"

SAMPLE for Lavender Sachet
Stitched on a purchased 18"-square natural linen handkerchief using Waste Canvas 14 over 1 thread, the finished design size is 2⅜" x 2⅜". The canvas was cut 5" x 5". Center and baste the canvas at a 45° angle on 1 corner of the handkerchief. Begin stitching 2½" from the corner and 1¼" from the edges of the handkerchief.

FABRICS	DESIGN SIZES
Aida 11	3⅛" x 3⅛"
Aida 14	2⅜" x 2⅜"
Aida 18	1⅞" x 1⅞"
Hardanger 22	1½" x 1½"

MATERIALS (for 1 sachet)

Completed cross-stitch on 18"-square natural
linen handkerchief
2¼ yards (1"-wide) double-edge ecru lace
Small bowl
2"-diameter Styrofoam ball
1 ounce of potpourri

For Pink Sachet:
1 cup of cold brewed coffee
2½ yards (⅛"-wide) pink ribbon;
matching thread

For Lavender Sachet:
1 cup of cranberry juice
2½ yards (⅛"-wide) lavender ribbon;
matching thread

For Dark Green Sachet:
1 cup of grape juice
2½ yards (⅛"-wide) dark green ribbon;
matching thread

Stitch Count: 39 x 39 (Pink Sachet)

Anchor		DMC (used for sample)	
Step 1: Cross-stitch (1 strand)			
868	⊠	3779	Terra Cotta-vy. lt.
76	⊠	3731	Dusty Rose-med.
70	○	3685	Mauve-dk.
108	–	211	Lavender-lt.
167	–	519	Sky Blue
203	○	954	Nile Green
246	●	986	Forest Green-vy. dk.
Step 2: Backstitch (1 strand)			
382		3021	Brown Gray-vy. dk.

DIRECTIONS

1. Cut lace into 4 (20") lengths. Center 1 length
of lace on hem on right side of handkerchief and
pin. Topstitch lace to handkerchief. Repeat with
remaining 3 lengths of trim, mitering corners.

2. Pour liquid into small bowl. Place handkerchief
in liquid, wetting fabric and lace thoroughly. Let
soak for 5–10 minutes or until color is set. (Color
will be lighter when fabric is dry.) Remove from
liquid, but do not wring. Place handkerchief flat
between several layers of paper towels or cotton
rags; press out excess moisture. Place clean rag
or terry-cloth towel over stitched area and iron
handkerchief until dry.

3. Make a small, loose knot in 1 end of ribbon.
Continue making knots at 1" intervals along
length of ribbon. Beginning at 1 corner of
handkerchief, slipstitch ribbon to center of trim
through all layers. Continue around handkerchief. Cut off excess ribbon and set it aside.
Tack raw edge of ribbon under first knot.

4. Place potpourri in center of right side of handkerchief. Place Styrofoam ball on top of potpourri.
Gather handkerchief loosely around ball and tie
with remaining ribbon.

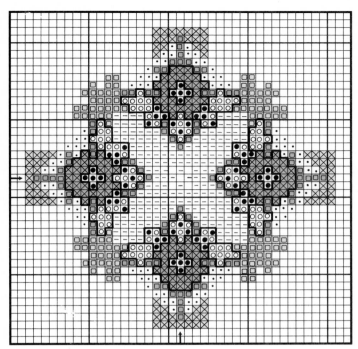

Stitch Count: 39 × 39 (Dark Green Sachet)

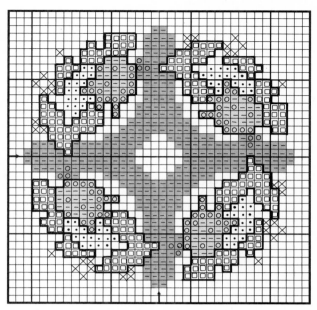

Stitch Count: 34 x 34 (Lavender Sachet)

Anchor		DMC (used for sample)	
		Step 1: Cross-stitch (2 strands)	
24	·	776	Pink-med.
76	☒	3731	Dusty Rose-med.
108	◩	211	Lavender-lt.
167	☒	519	Sky Blue
840	◩	3768	Slate Green-dk.
242	○	989	Forest Green
246	●	986	Forest Green-vy. dk.
397	–	3072	Beaver Gray-vy. lt.
		Step 2: Backstitch (1 strand)	
382	⌐	3021	Brown Gray-vy. dk.

Anchor		DMC (used for sample)	
		Step 1: Cross-stitch (1 strand)	
868	–	3779	Terra Cotta-vy. lt.
338	○	3776	Mahogany-lt.
70	☒	3685	Mauve-dk.
108	▨	211	Lavender-lt.
158	·	747	Sky Blue-vy. lt.
206	□	955	Nile Green-lt.
205	◉	911	Emerald Green-med.
		Step 2: Backstitch (1 strand)	
840	⌐	3768	Slate Green-dk.

Box Band

SAMPLE

Stitched on cream Belfast Linen 32 over 2 threads, the finished design size is 5" x 3½" for 1 motif. The fabric was cut 30" x 10". The number of motifs varies according to the size of the box used. The sample is shown on an 8" x 4½" x 4" box (excluding feet and box top) and uses 3½ motifs. The bold lines on the graph indicate repeats. See Suppliers for Mill Hill Beads.

FABRICS	DESIGN SIZES (for 1 motif)
Aida 11	7¼" x 5⅛"
Aida 14	5¾" x 4"
Aida 18	4½" x 3⅛"
Hardanger 22	3⅝" x 2½"

MATERIALS

Completed cross-stitch on cream Belfast Linen 32; matching thread
Box

DIRECTIONS

All seam allowances are ¼".

1. With right sides facing and raw edges aligned, fold design piece in half. Stitch long edge, leaving ends open. Turn. Center seam in back and design in front; press.

2. Measure around box. With design centered, trim ends of design piece to this measurement, plus 1". With right sides facing, stitch ends together. Turn. Slip band over box.

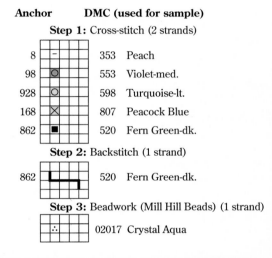

Anchor		DMC (used for sample)	
Step 1: Cross-stitch (2 strands)			
8	–	353	Peach
98	◎	553	Violet-med.
928	○	598	Turquoise-lt.
168	✕	807	Peacock Blue
862	■	520	Fern Green-dk.
Step 2: Backstitch (1 strand)			
862		520	Fern Green-dk.
Step 3: Beadwork (Mill Hill Beads) (1 strand)			
	∴	02017	Crystal Aqua

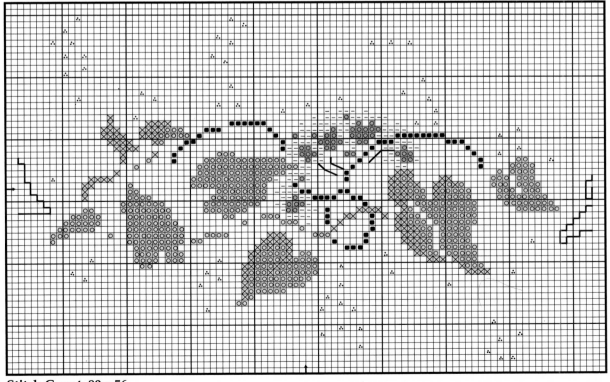

Stitch Count: 80 x 56

Crystal Jar Lids

SAMPLE for Small Lid

Stitched on white Belfast Linen 32 over 2 threads, the finished design size is 2" x 2". The fabric was cut 8" x 8". See Suppliers for crystal jar with lid.

FABRICS	DESIGN SIZES
Aida 11	3" x 3"
Aida 14	2⅜" x 2⅜"
Aida 18	1⅞" x 1⅞"
Hardanger 22	1½" x 1½"

SAMPLE for Large Lid

Stitched on white Belfast Linen 32 over 2 threads, the finished design size is 2¾" x 2¾". The fabric was cut 9" x 9". See Suppliers for crystal jar with lid.

FABRICS	DESIGN SIZES
Aida 11	4⅛" x 4"
Aida 14	3¼" x 3⅛"
Aida 18	2½" x 2⅜"
Hardanger 22	2" x 2"

MATERIALS (for 1 lid)

Completed cross-stitch on white Belfast Linen 32
Scrap of fleece
Crystal jar with lid

DIRECTIONS

1. With design centered, trim fabric to 2⅞"-diameter circle (for small lid) or 3⅞"-diameter circle (for large lid). Trim fleece to match design piece.

2. Insert fleece and design piece in jar lid according to manufacturer's instructions.

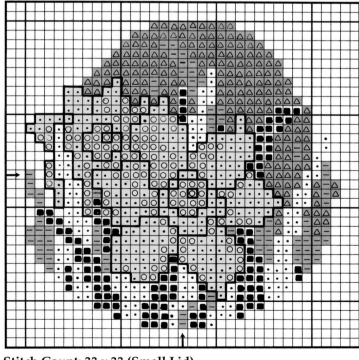

Anchor		DMC (used for sample)	

Step 1: Cross-stitch (1 strand)

300	·	745	Yellow-lt. pale
297	O	743	Yellow-med.
48	△	818	Baby Pink
875	–	503	Blue Green-med.
214	·	368	Pistachio Green-lt.
216	■	367	Pistachio Green-dk.

Step 2: Backstitch (1 strand)

| 337 | ⌐ | 3778 | Terra Cotta |

Stitch Count: 33 x 33 (Small Lid)

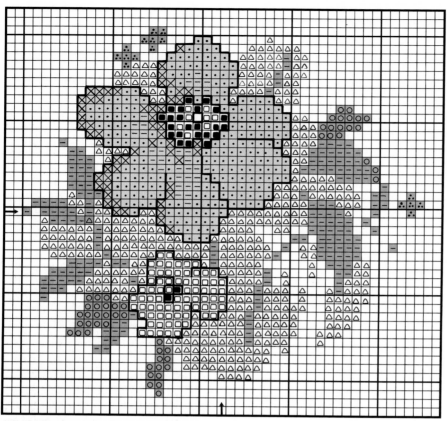

Stitch Count: 45 x 43 (Large Lid)

Anchor   **DMC (used for sample)**

Step 1: Cross-stitch (1 strand)

8		353	Peach
49		3689	Mauve-lt.
66		3688	Mauve-med.
968		3727	Antique Mauve-lt.
969		316	Antique Mauve-med.
970		3726	Antique Mauve-dk.
214		368	Pistachio Green-lt.
216		367	Pistachio Green-dk.
376		842	Beige Brown-vy. lt.

Step 2: Backstitch (1 strand)

| 66 | | 3688 | Mauve-med. (small pink flower) |
| 970 | | 3726 | Antique Mauve-dk. (large flower) |

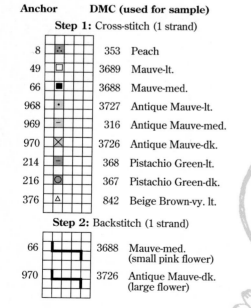

Photo Album Band

SAMPLE

Stitched on Belfast Linen 32 over 2 threads, the finished design size is 3⅜" x 2½" for 1 motif. The fabric was cut 18" x 18". Begin stitching in the center of the fabric 1" from the left edge. Repeat the motif 4 times (bold lines on the graph indicate placement for the repeat).

FABRICS	DESIGN SIZES
Aida 11	4⅞" x 3¾"
Aida 14	3⅞" x 2⅞"
Aida 18	3" x 2¼"
Hardanger 22	2½" x 1⅞"

MATERIALS

Completed cross-stitch on cream Belfast Linen 32
1 (9" x 14") photo album with removable covers
Ice pick or other sharp instrument to punch ¼" hole in front cover
¾ yard (2½"-wide) white tatted or crocheted beading
½ yard (1"-wide) white tatted or crocheted trim
1¼ yards (½"-wide) ivory satin ribbon
Liquid ravel preventer
1¼ yards (¼") ivory cording
Hot-glue gun and glue sticks

DIRECTIONS

1. Remove cover of photo album. Measure 3" up from bottom edge and ¾" in from spine of cover; mark position. Repeat for top edge. Punch 1 hole through each mark for decorative cording. Set aside.

2. To make band, with design centered, trim design piece to 16" x 6½". With right sides facing and raw edges aligned, stitch together along long edges. Turn. Center design in front and seam in back; press.

3. From 2½" beading, cut 1 (16") length and 1 (7") length. From ribbon, cut 1 (16") length, 2 (11") lengths, and 1 (7") length.

4. Weave matching length of ribbon through each length of beading. Treat all ends of ribbon and beading with liquid ravel preventer and set aside.

5. Referring to photo, center and glue 1 (11") ribbon horizontally across cover, about ¾" from top edge. Wrap excess ribbon around edges of cover and glue to underside. Glue remaining 11" ribbon ¼" below first ribbon in same manner.

6. Position 16" length of beading vertically on right edge of cover, about ¼" from edge and glue in same manner.

Place 7" length of beading diagonally across bottom left corner of cover and glue in same manner.

7. Referring to photo, position design piece diagonally across cover and glue in same manner.

8. Glue 1"-wide trim along top edge of design piece in same manner.

9. From underside of cover, thread cording through punched holes in cover. Tie cord into a bow on top of cover and knot each end. Replace cover on album.

114

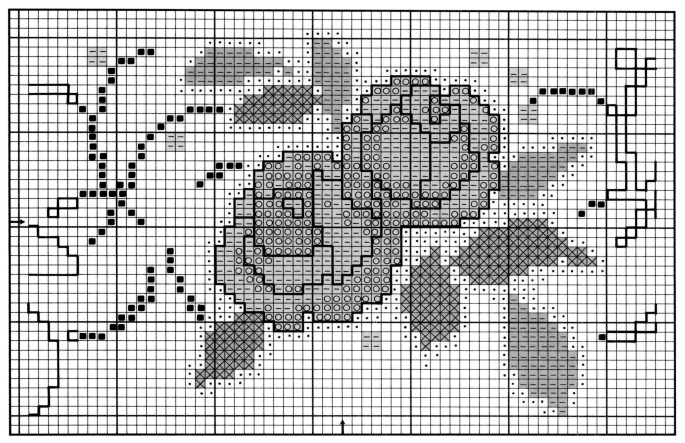

Stitch Count: 54 x 41

Anchor   **DMC** (used for sample)

Step 1: Cross-stitch (2 strands)

301	•	744	Yellow-pale
49	−	3689	Mauve-lt.
66	○	3688	Mauve-med.
159	■	3325	Baby Blue-lt.
210	−	562	Jade-med.
212	✕	561	Jade-vy. dk.

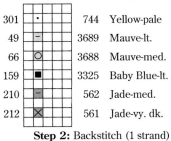

Step 2: Backstitch (1 strand)

| 70 | ⌐ | 3685 | Mauve-dk. |

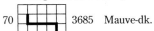

Lacy Hearts

SAMPLE for Heart with Pansies

Stitched on cream Belfast Linen 32 over 2 threads, the finished design size is 5⅝" x 4½". The fabric was cut 12" x 11".

FABRICS	DESIGN SIZES
Aida 11	8⅛" x 6⅝"
Aida 14	6⅜" x 5¼"
Aida 18	5" x 4"
Hardanger 22	4⅛" x 3⅜"

SAMPLE for Heart with Violets

Stitched on cream Belfast Linen 32 over 2 threads, the finished design size is 5¾" x 4⅜". The fabric was cut 12" x 11".

FABRICS	DESIGN SIZES
Aida 11	8⅜" x 6⅜"
Aida 14	6⅝" x 5"
Aida 18	5⅛" x 3⅞"
Hardanger 22	4⅛" x 3⅛"

MATERIALS (for 1 heart)

Completed cross-stitch on cream Belfast Linen 32; matching thread
7" x 6" piece of green crushed velvet; matching thread
Polyester stuffing

For Heart with Pansies:
½ yard (1½"-wide) pre-gathered ecru lace
¾ yard (⅛"-wide) flat gold braid
Gold filament thread

For Heart with Violets:
½ yard (2"-wide) pre-gathered flat gold metallic lace
¾ yard (1/16"-wide) violet braid; matching thread
¾ yard (1/16"-wide) smooth violet cord

DIRECTIONS

All seam allowances are ¼".

1. For heart front, cut out design piece ¼" from edge of design. Using design piece as pattern, cut 1 heart from green velvet for back.

2. With right sides facing, raw edges aligned, and beginning at bottom point of heart, stitch lace to design piece. Trim excess at point of heart. Slip-stitch ends of lace together.

3. With right sides facing, raw edges aligned, and lace sandwiched between, stitch front to back along stitching line of lace, leaving an opening for turning. Turn. Stuff firmly. Slipstitch opening closed.

4. For Heart with Pansies: From gold braid, cut 1 (16") length and 1 (10") length. Using gold thread, slipstitch 16" length along edges of design piece, beginning and ending at top center of heart (see photo). To make hanger, fold 10" length in half. Handling ends as 1, fold ends under ½". Using gold thread, stitch folded ends to top center of heart back.

5. For Heart with Violets: From violet braid and violet cord, cut 1 (18") length and 1 (10") length from each. To make trim, twist 1 (18") length of cord and braid together; slipstitch trim along edges of design piece, beginning and ending at top center of heart (see photo). To make hanger, twist remaining 10" lengths together. Slipstitch each end with thread. Fold braid in half and knot ends together. Stitch knot to top center of heart back.

Stitch Count: 90 x 73 (Heart with Pansies)

Anchor   DMC (used for sample)

Step 1: Cross-stitch (2 strands)

1	+	White
295	·	726 Topaz-lt.
891	I	676 Old Gold-lt.
901	○	680 Old Gold-dk.
10	△	351 Coral
11	✕	350 Coral-med.
13	∴	347 Salmon-vy. dk.
323	+	722 Orange Spice-lt.
42	○	3350 Dusty Rose-dk.
43	●	815 Garnet-med.
95	–	554 Violet-lt.
99	✕	552 Violet-dk.
110	□	208 Lavender-vy. dk.
119	∴	3746 Blue Violet-dk.
265	•	3348 Yellow Green-lt.
214	□	368 Pistachio Green-lt.
861	✕	3363 Pine Green-med.
210	△	562 Jade-med.
879	◀	500 Blue Green-vy. dk.
349	⊡	301 Mahogany-med.
355	∴	975 Golden Brown-dk.
380	╲	839 Beige Brown-dk.
382	■	3371 Black Brown

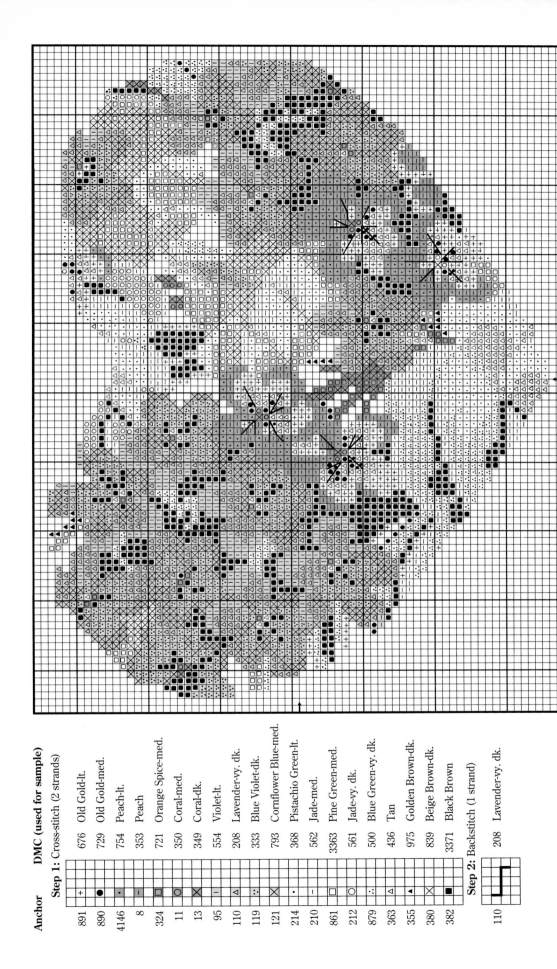

Stitch Count: 92 x 70 (Heart with Violets)

Anchor	DMC (used for sample)	
Step 1: Cross-stitch (2 strands)		
891	+	676	Old Gold-lt.
890	●	729	Old Gold-med.
4146	⊡	754	Peach-lt.
8			353	Peach
324	▣	721	Orange Spice-med.
11	○	350	Coral-med.
13	✕	349	Coral-dk.
95	−	554	Violet-lt.
110	◁	208	Lavender-vy. dk.
119	⦂⦂	333	Blue Violet-dk.
121	✕	793	Cornflower Blue-med.
214	·	368	Pistachio Green-lt.
210	−	562	Jade-med.
861	☐	3363	Pine Green-med.
212	○	561	Jade-vy. dk.
879	⦂⦂	500	Blue Green-vy. dk.
363	◁	436	Tan
355	▲	975	Golden Brown-dk.
380	✕	839	Beige Brown-dk.
382	■	3371	Black Brown

Step 2: Backstitch (1 strand)		
110		208	Lavender-vy. dk.

Small Sachet Pillows

SAMPLE
Stitched on cream Linda 27 over 2 threads, the finished design size is ⅝" x ⅝" for 1 motif. The fabric was cut 13" x 3" for each band. Stitch 12 motifs for each band (bold lines on the graph indicate placement for repeats). See Suppliers for Mill Hill Beads.

FABRICS	DESIGN SIZES
Aida 11	⅞" x ⅞"
Aida 14	⅝" x ⅝"
Aida 18	½" x ½"
Hardanger 22	⅜" x ⅜"

MATERIALS (for Sleeve Sachet)
Completed cross-stitch on cream Linda 27; matching thread
Liquid ravel preventer
¼ yard of satin brocade fabric; matching thread
⅝ yard (⅝"-wide) cream lace trim, cut in half
1 yard (⅛"-wide) ecru ribbon
⅛"-wide ribbon: 12" each of burgundy, rose
¼ yard of white-on-cream striped satin fabric; matching thread
Polyester stuffing
1 ounce of potpourri

DIRECTIONS
All seam allowances are ¼".

1. With design centered, trim design piece to 11¼" x 1". Apply liquid ravel preventer to raw edges. Cut 2 (11¼") lengths from ecru ribbon. From brocade fabric, cut 1 (11¼" x 8¾") piece. From striped fabric, cut 1 (11" x 8½") piece; set aside.

2. To make sleeve, with right sides facing and raw edges aligned, fold brocade in half widthwise.

Stitch side and 1 end, leaving other end open. Do not turn. Turn raw edge under ¼" and stitch narrow hem. Turn under another 1½" and stitch. Turn sleeve; set aside.

3. Topstitch 1 length of lace trim to 1 long edge on right side of design piece. Repeat with remaining length of trim on opposite edge of design piece. Slipstitch 1 (11¼") length of ribbon over edge of lace, covering topstitching. Repeat with second length of ribbon.

4. Beginning and ending at side seam, pin top edge of design piece to sleeve 1" from open end. Turn under ends of design piece and slipstitch long edges and ends of design piece to sleeve.

5. Cut remaining ecru ribbon in half. Holding both lengths together as 1, tie a double bow. Knot ends and tack to bottom edge of design piece at sleeve seam.

6. To make gathered ribbon rosebuds, cut burgundy and rose ribbons in half. Tie knot in 1 end of 1 length. At opposite end of ribbon, fray ribbon with fingernail and pull 1 or 2 threads from center, pushing ribbon back to bunch against knot. Tack ends together to make a circle. Repeat with remaining lengths of ribbon. Tack rosebuds to center of bow.

7. To make sachet pillow, with right sides facing and raw edges aligned, fold striped fabric in half widthwise. Stitch side and 1 end, leaving other end open. Turn. Fill half of pillow loosely with stuffing. Fill remainder of pillow loosely with potpourri. Turn under seam allowance and slipstitch end closed. Insert pillow in sleeve.

MATERIALS (for Bolster Sachet)
Completed cross-stitch on cream Linda 27;
 matching thread
Liquid ravel preventer
¼ yard of satin brocade fabric; matching thread
⅝ yard (⅝"-wide) cream lace trim, cut in half
2 yards (⅛"-wide) ecru ribbon
⅛"-wide ribbon: 1 yard each of burgundy, rose
¾ yard (5"-wide) cream lace trim; matching thread
2–3 ounces of potpourri

DIRECTIONS
All seam allowances are ¼".

1. With design centered, trim design piece to
11¼" x 1". Apply liquid ravel preventer to raw
edges. Cut 2 (11¼") lengths of ecru ribbon. From
brocade fabric, cut 1 (11¼" x 8½") piece. From 5"-
wide lace trim, cut 2 (11") lengths; set aside.

2. To make bolster, with right sides facing and
raw edges aligned, fold brocade fabric in half
widthwise. Stitch along 8½" edge, leaving ends
open. Turn.

3. Repeat Step 3 of sleeve sachet to finish long
edges of design piece. Beginning and ending at
seam, pin design piece to center of bolster, turning
under and overlapping ends of design piece at
bolster seam. Slipstitch long edges and ends of
design piece to bolster.

4. Slipstitch 1 length of 5"-wide lace to 1 end of
bolster. Slipstitch cut edges of lace together.
Repeat at opposite end.

5. Cut remaining ecru ribbon into 4 equal lengths;
knot all ends. Handling 2 lengths as 1, tie ribbons
around 1 open end of bolster over stitching line of
lace and fabric, gathering fabric securely, and then
tie a double bow. Stuff bolster loosely with potpourri. Tie remaining 2 ribbons at opposite end of
bolster in same manner.

6. Cut each ⅛"-wide ribbon into 6 (6") lengths. To
make gathered ribbon rosebuds, see Step 6 of
sleeve sachet. Tack 6 rosebuds to center of
each bow.

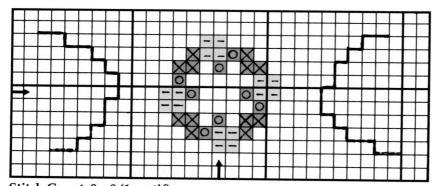

Stitch Count: 9 x 9 (1 motif)

Anchor		DMC (used for sample)	
		Step 1: Cross-stitch (2 strands)	
875	◯	503	Blue Green-med.
878	✕	501	Blue Green-dk.
		Step 2: Beadwork (Mill Hill Beads)	
	–	03005	

122

Handmade Hand Towel

SAMPLE

Stitched on moss green Murano 30 over 2 threads, the finished design size is 6⅞" x 2⅝". The fabric was cut 20" x 9".

FABRICS	DESIGN SIZES
Aida 11	9⅜" x 3½"
Aida 14	7⅜" x 2¾"
Aida 18	5¾" x 2⅛"
Hardanger 22	4⅝" x 1¾"

MATERIALS

Completed cross-stitch on moss green Murano 30; matching thread

½ yard unstitched ash rose Murano 30; matching thread

7 small heart- and star-shaped novelty buttons (optional)

1 yard (⅛"-wide) green satin ribbon (optional)

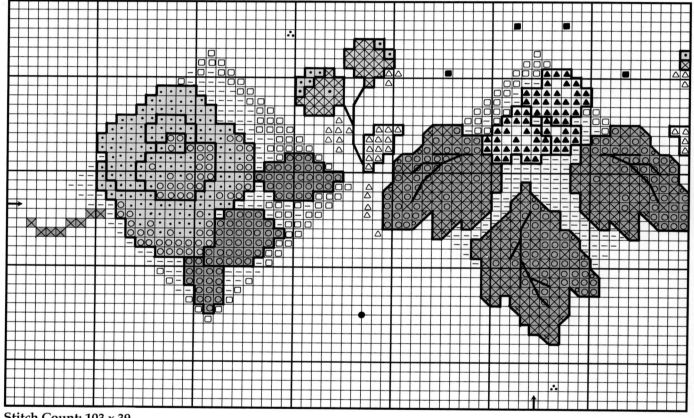

Stitch Count: 103 x 39

124

DIRECTIONS

1. With design centered, trim design piece to 18¼" x 4". Turn long edges under ¼" and press. From ash rose Murano, cut 1 (18" x 29¾") piece for towel.

2. If desired, embellish design piece by tacking buttons around design area (see photo). Also, if desired, cut ribbon into 4 equal lengths. Knot all ends. Holding 2 lengths together as 1, tie into a bow. Repeat to make second bow. Tack to design piece (see photo).

3. Position design piece horizontally on towel, with bottom edge of design piece 3½" from bottom raw edge of towel and left and right edges aligned (see photo). Slipstitch edges of design piece to towel.

4. Zigzag raw edges of towel. Turn under ¼" twice along all edges and stitch hem.

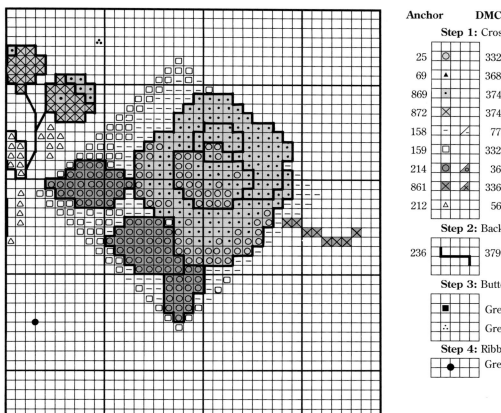

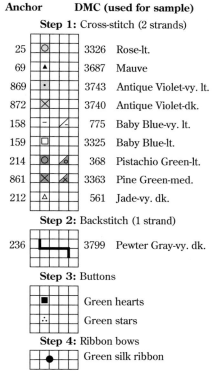

Anchor		DMC	(used for sample)
Step 1:	Cross-stitch (2 strands)		
25	○	3326	Rose-lt.
69	▲	3687	Mauve
869	·	3743	Antique Violet-vy. lt.
872	✕	3740	Antique Violet-dk.
158	– ╱	775	Baby Blue-vy. lt.
159	□	3325	Baby Blue-lt.
214	○ ◢	368	Pistachio Green-lt.
861	✕ ◹	3363	Pine Green-med.
212	△	561	Jade-vy. dk.

Step 2: Backstitch (1 strand)

236	⌐	3799	Pewter Gray-vy. dk.

Step 3: Buttons

■	Green hearts
∴	Green stars

Step 4: Ribbon bows

●	Green silk ribbon

Beaded Brooches

SAMPLE for Fanciful Fleur-de-lis

Stitched on cream Plastic Canvas 14 over 1 bar, the finished design size is 2½" x 3⅝". The canvas was cut 4" x 4". After stitching, cut along bold line (see graph). Overcast-stitch edges of design piece. Tack or glue pin back to back of design piece. See Suppliers for Mill Hill Beads.

SAMPLE for Blooming Blossom

Stitched on cream Plastic Canvas 14 over 1 bar, the finished design size is 3⅛" x 3¼". The canvas was cut 4" x 4". After stitching, cut along bold line (see graph). Overcast-stitch edges of design piece. Tack or glue pin back to back of design piece. See Suppliers for Mill Hill Beads.

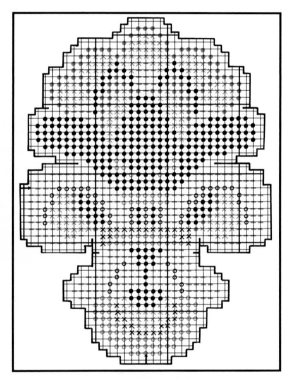

Stitch Count: 35 x 50 (Fanciful Fleur-de-lis)

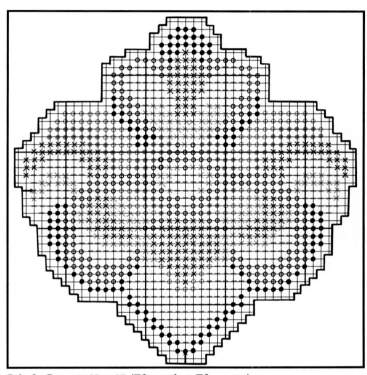

Stitch Count: 43 x 45 (Blooming Blossom)

Mill Hill Beads (used for sample)

Step 1: Beadwork

⊙	00557	Gold
✖	00165	Christmas Red
-	00968	Red
✳	03003	Antique Cranberry
⊙	00561	Ice Green
●	03029	Autumn Green
●	00221	Bronze

Mill Hill Beads (used for sample)

Step 1: Beadwork

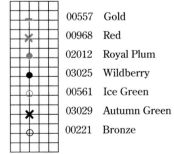

-	00557	Gold
✳	00968	Red
●	02012	Royal Plum
●	03025	Wildberry
⊙	00561	Ice Green
✖	03029	Autumn Green
⊙	00221	Bronze

Anchor   DMC (used for sample)

Step 2: Cut and overcast (8 strands)

375

420   Hazel Nut Brown-dk.
         DMC Floss

Anchor   DMC (used for sample)

Step 2: Cut and Overcast (8 strands)

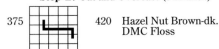

375

420   Hazel Nut Brown-dk.
         DMC Floss

Hatband Border

SAMPLE

Stitched on amber Linen 28 over 1 thread, the finished design size is 6⅛" x 2½" for 1 repeat. The fabric was cut 32" x 32". Begin stitching in the center of the fabric 1½" from the left edge. Repeat the motif 4 times (bold lines on the graph indicate placement for repeat).

FABRICS	DESIGN SIZES
Aida 11	7⅞" x 3⅜"
Aida 14	6⅛" x 2⅝"
Aida 18	4¾" x 2"
Hardanger 22	3⅞" x 1⅝"

MATERIALS

Completed cross-stitch on amber Linen 28; matching thread
1 (5" x 32") piece of non-fusible interfacing
Hat
Mauve velvet flower with leaves, plastic grapes or berries, scrap of dark maroon netting

DIRECTIONS

1. To make band, with design centered, trim design piece to measure 5" x 32". Zigzag interfacing to wrong side of design piece.

With right sides facing and raw edges aligned, fold strip in half lengthwise and stitch long edges together, leaving ends open. Turn. Center seam in back and design in front; press.

2. Beginning and ending at front of hat, slipstitch top of band in place around brim, folding end of band to form a loop (see photo).

3. Referring to photo, tack flower, fruit, and netting to front of hat.

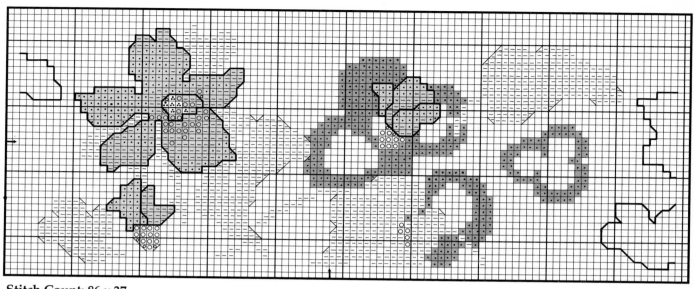

Stitch Count: 86 x 37

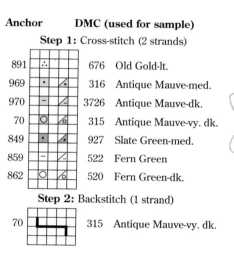

Anchor			DMC (used for sample)
Step 1: Cross-stitch (2 strands)			
891			676 Old Gold-lt.
969			316 Antique Mauve-med.
970			3726 Antique Mauve-dk.
70			315 Antique Mauve-vy. dk.
849			927 Slate Green-med.
859			522 Fern Green
862			520 Fern Green-dk.
Step 2: Backstitch (1 strand)			
70			315 Antique Mauve-vy. dk.

SAMPLE for Pincushion

Stitched on cream Plastic Canvas 14 over 1 bar, the finished design size is 1⅞" x 1⅞". The canvas was cut 4" x 4" for 1 design. Stitch 2. After stitching, cut along bold lines (see graph). See Suppliers for Mill Hill Beads.

MATERIALS (for Pincushion)

2 completed design pieces on cream Plastic Canvas 14
Scrap of polyester fleece
⅝ yard (⅛"-wide) light peach satin ribbon; matching thread

DIRECTIONS

1. Cut 2 (1½"-square) pieces of fleece. Stack 1 design piece (right side down), 2 fleece pieces, and second design piece (right side up). Overcast-stitch all edges.

2. Tie small bow in ends of ribbon, making large loop. Tack bow to 1 corner of pincushion.

SAMPLE for Needle Case

Stitched on cream Plastic Canvas 14 over 1 bar, the finished design size is 1⅞" x 2½" for front and back pieces and ¼" x 2½" for spine. The canvas was cut 4" x 5" for front and back pieces and 3" x 5" for spine. After stitching, cut along bold lines (see graph). See Suppliers for Mill Hill Beads.

MATERIALS (for Needle Case)

3 completed design pieces on cream Plastic Canvas 14
Scrap of brown felt
⅜ yard (⅛"-wide) light peach satin ribbon
Thick craft glue

DIRECTIONS

1. Overcast-stitch top, right, and bottom edges of front design piece. Overcast-stitch top, left, and bottom edges of back design piece. Overcast-stitch right edge of spine to left edge of front design piece. Overcast-stitch left edge of spine to right edge of back design piece.

2. From ribbon, cut 2 (6½") lengths. From felt, cut 2 (1¾" x 2⅜") pieces.

3. To make ties, on wrong side of front design piece, center 1 end of 1 length of ribbon on long outer edge; glue. Glue remaining length of ribbon on wrong side of back design piece in same manner.

4. Glue 1 felt piece to wrong side of front design piece along edges only (do not apply glue to center of felt). Glue remaining felt piece to wrong side of back design piece in same manner.

SAMPLE for Scissors Holder

Stitched on cream Plastic Canvas 14 over 1 bar, the finished design size is 1⅞" x 3½". The canvas was cut 4" x 6" for 1 design. Stitch 2. After stitching, cut along bold lines (see graph). Overcast-stitch edges above the double line on each design piece (see graph). With wrong sides facing, stack the 2 design pieces and overcast-stitch edges together below the double line. See Suppliers for Mill Hill Beads.

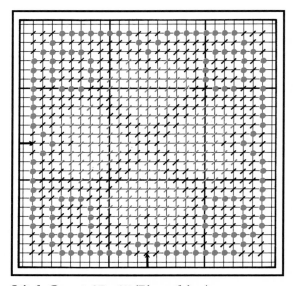

Stitch Count: 27 x 27 (Pincushion)

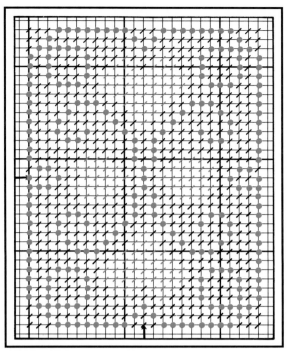

Stitch Count: 27 x 35 (Needle Case Front)

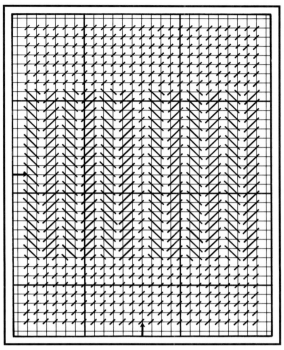

Stitch Count: 27 x 35 (Needle Case Back)

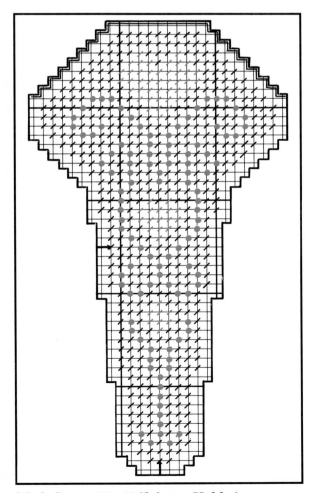

Stitch Count: 27 x 49 (Scissors Holder)

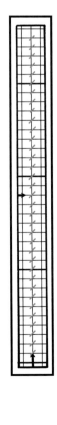

Stitch Count: 1 x 35 (Needle Case Spine)

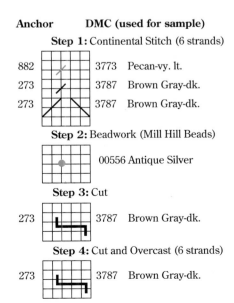

Anchor		DMC (used for sample)	
	Step 1: Continental Stitch (6 strands)		
882		3773	Pecan-vy. lt.
273		3787	Brown Gray-dk.
273		3787	Brown Gray-dk.
	Step 2: Beadwork (Mill Hill Beads)		
		00556 Antique Silver	
	Step 3: Cut		
273		3787	Brown Gray-dk.
	Step 4: Cut and Overcast (6 strands)		
273		3787	Brown Gray-dk.

White Fringe Sachets

SAMPLE for Peach Flower Sachet
Stitched on white Belfast Linen 32 over 2 threads, the finished design size is 2½" x 2½". The fabric was cut 9" x 9".

FABRICS	DESIGN SIZES
Aida 11	3⅝" x 3⅝"
Aida 14	2⅞" x 2⅞"
Aida 18	2¼" x 2¼"
Hardanger 22	1⅞" x 1⅞"

SAMPLE for Pink Flower Sachet
Stitched on white Belfast Linen 32 over 2 threads, the finished design size is 2" x 2⅛". The fabric was cut 9" x 9".

FABRICS	DESIGN SIZES
Aida 11	3" x 3⅛"
Aida 14	2⅜" x 2⅜"
Aida 18	1⅞" x 1⅞"
Hardanger 22	1½" x 1½"

MATERIALS (for 1 sachet)
Completed cross-stitch on white Belfast Linen 32; matching thread
Tracing paper
1 (8-ounce) bag of potpourri
¼ yard (⅛"-wide) pink satin ribbon
2 small pink glass beads
Scrap of green variegated satin ribbon
For Peach Flower Sachet:
1 (7" x 10") piece of unstitched white Belfast Linen 32
¼ yard (4"-wide) white fringe
1⅝ yards (½"-wide) flat white braid
1 medium pink satin ribbon rose
For Pink Flower Sachet:
½ yard of bridal netting
⅛ yard (4"-wide) white fringe
1 yard (½"-wide) flat white braid
3 medium pink satin ribbon roses

DIRECTIONS (for Peach Flower Sachet)
The pattern includes ¼" seam allowances.

1. For bag front, trace pattern. Position pattern on design area as shown on pattern and transfer to design piece; cut out. For bag back, transfer pattern to unstitched linen and cut out.

2. With right sides facing and raw edges aligned, stitch front to back, leaving top open for turning. Turn.

3. Referring to photo, topstitch fringe to bottom edge of bag front. Trim excess fringe.

4. Cut 2 (16") lengths of flat white braid. Beginning and ending at top of bag, slipstitch 1 length of braid along edges of bag front, covering edges of fringe. Slipstitch second length of braid along edges of bag back.

5. Stuff bag with potpourri up to bottom of bag neck. Pinch top of bag and wrap tightly with thread from bottom of neck to within ⅛" of bag top.

6. From braid, cut 1 (3") length, 1 (12") length, and 1 (9") length. Slipstitch 3" length across top of bag, covering raw edges.

7. To make hanger, stitch 1 end of 12" length of braid to top center of bag front and other end to top center of bag back. Wrap remaining 9" length of braid around bag neck, covering thread wraps and raw edges of hanger. Tack end in place.

8. Tie pink ribbon in a bow around bag neck below braid. Thread glass beads onto ends of ribbon and knot ribbon ends to secure. To make leaves, cut 2 (1½") pieces of green variegated ribbon. Fold each piece of ribbon in half and tack ends to bow (see photo). Center ribbon rose over leaves and tack in place.

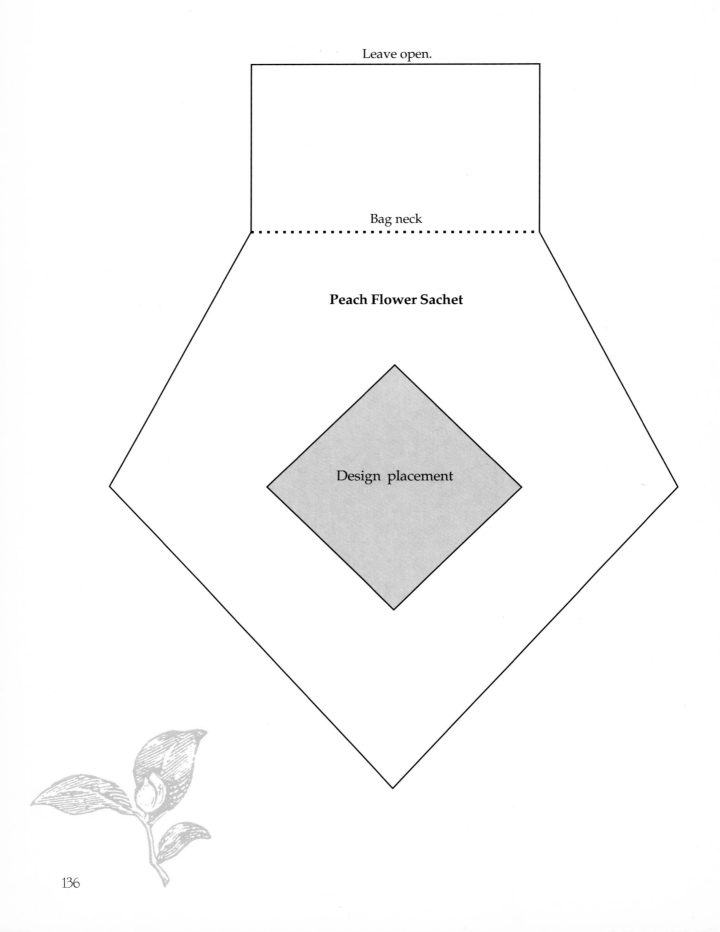

Leave open.

Bag neck

Peach Flower Sachet

Design placement

DIRECTIONS (for Pink Flower Sachet)

The pattern includes ¼" seam allowances.

1. Trace pattern. Position pattern on design area as shown on pattern and transfer to design piece; cut out.

2. With right sides facing and raw edges aligned, fold bag in half lengthwise. Stitch center back and bottom seam, leaving top edge open. Turn. Fold fabric so that design is centered on front.

3. From netting, cut 1 (20" x 14") piece. Fold in half and stitch long edge to make 10" x 14" tube. Turn. Run a gathering thread around bottom 10" edge of tube, ¼" from edge. Place linen bag inside tube, matching bottom edges. Pull thread to gather, easing fullness so design shows through netting. Baste netting to bag at bottom edge. Trim excess netting to match bottom angle of bag.

4. Cut 1 (3½") length of fringe. Stitch fringe over netting along bottom edge of bag front. Cut 1 (9") length of braid and topstitch around front and back bottom edge of bag, covering raw edges of fringe.

5. To make hanger, cut 1 (12") length of braid. Stitch 1 end of braid inside linen bag top at center front and other end to center back.

6. Stuff linen bag with potpourri to within 1½" of top. Run a gathering stitch around top of linen bag. Pull thread tightly to close bag. Secure thread. Fold top edge of netting 2" to inside. Pinch netting and wrap tightly with thread, securing netting ends and hanger. Arrange fullness of netting to make puffs at top of bag (see photo).

7. Cut remaining braid into 1 (4") length, 1 (5") length, and 1 (6") length. Fold 5" and 6" lengths in half and tack ends of loops to neck of bag on left side. Wrap 4" length around bag top, covering thread wraps; tack end in place.

8. Tie pink ribbon in a bow and tack to braid loop on left side of bag. Thread glass beads onto ends of ribbon and knot ribbon ends to secure. To make leaves, cut 5 (1½") pieces of green variegated ribbon. Fold each piece of ribbon in half and tack ends to braid. Center ribbon roses over leaves and tack in place.

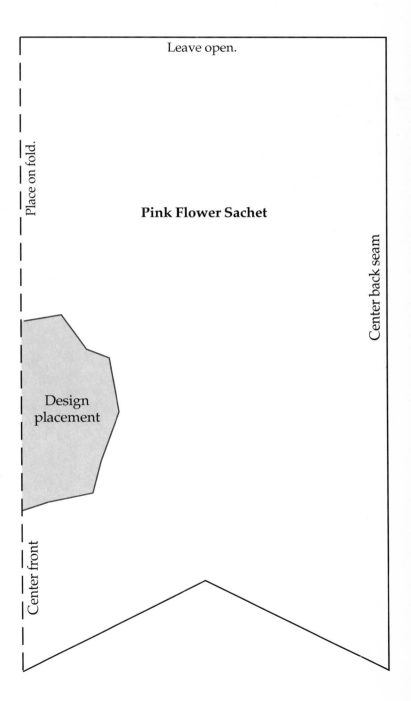

Leave open.

Place on fold.

Pink Flower Sachet

Center back seam

Design placement

Center front

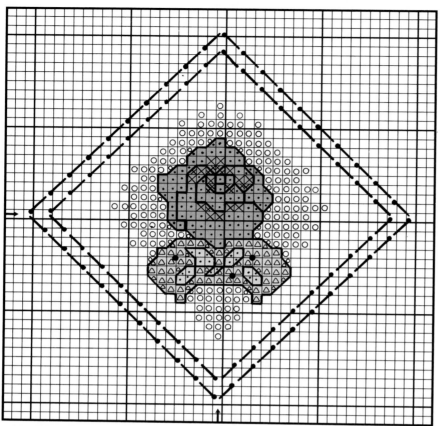

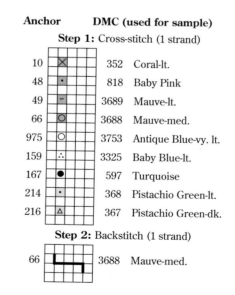

Anchor			DMC (used for sample)	
	Step 1: Cross-stitch (1 strand)			
300	△	◹	745	Yellow-lt. pale
8	⊡	◹	353	Peach
10	⊠	◸	352	Coral-lt.
975	○	◹	3753	Antique Blue-vy. lt.
214	⊡	◹	368	Pistachio Green-lt.
	Step 2: Backstitch (1 strand)			
10			3712	Salmon-med. (flower)
11			350	Coral-med. (flower base)
214			368	Pistachio Green-lt. (leaves)
	Step 3: Faggot Stitch (1 strand)			
1				White
	Step 4: French Knot (1 strand)			
214	●		368	Pistachio Green-lt.

Stitch Count: 40 x 40 (Peach Flower Sachet)

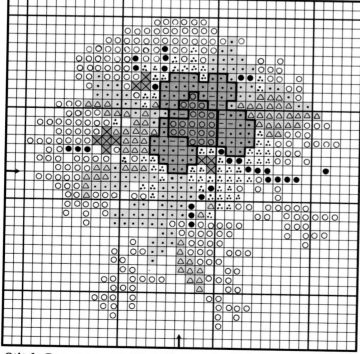

Anchor		DMC (used for sample)	
	Step 1: Cross-stitch (1 strand)		
10	⊠	352	Coral-lt.
48	⊡	818	Baby Pink
49	−	3689	Mauve-lt.
66	⊙	3688	Mauve-med.
975	○	3753	Antique Blue-vy. lt.
159	∴	3325	Baby Blue-lt.
167	●	597	Turquoise
214	·	368	Pistachio Green-lt.
216	△	367	Pistachio Green-dk.
	Step 2: Backstitch (1 strand)		
66		3688	Mauve-med.

Stitch Count: 33 x 34 (Pink Flower Sachet)

General Instructions

CROSS-STITCH GUIDELINES

Fabrics: Most designs in this book are worked on even-weave fabrics made especially for cross-stitch and can be found in your local needlework shop. If you cannot find a particular fabric, see Suppliers for ordering information. In sample paragraphs, fabrics used for models are identified by color, name, and thread count per inch.

Preparing Fabric: Cut fabric at least 3" larger on all sides than finished design size, or cut as indicated in sample information, to ensure enough space for matting, framing, and other finishing techniques. To prevent fraying, whipstitch or machine-zigzag raw edges or apply liquid ravel preventer.

Needles: Needles should slip easily through fabric holes but not pierce fabric. For fabric with 11 or fewer threads per inch, use needle size 24; for 14 threads per inch, use needle size 24 or 26; for 18 or more threads per inch, use needle size 26. Never leave needle in design area of fabric. It may leave rust or a permanent impression on fabric.

Floss: All numbers and color names are cross-referenced between Anchor and DMC brands of floss, except where noted. Cut floss into 18" lengths; longer pieces tend to twist and knot. For best coverage, separate strands. Dampen with wet sponge to straighten. Then put back together number of strands called for in color code. If floss becomes twisted, suspend needle and allow floss to unwind itself.

Centering Design: To find center of fabric, fold it in half from top to bottom and then from left to right. The intersection of folds is center. To find center of graph, follow vertical and horizontal arrows until they intersect. Begin stitching center of design at center of fabric or as noted in directions.

Securing Floss: Bring needle and most of floss up through fabric, holding a 1" tail of floss behind fabric where first stitches will be taken. Work first 4 or 5 stitches over tail of floss to secure it.

You can also use waste knot method. After tying a knot at end of floss, bring needle down through fabric about 1" from where first stitch will be taken. Plan placement of waste knot so that first 4 or 5 stitches will cover and secure 1" of floss on back of fabric, as described above. After floss is secured, cut off knot.

To secure floss when finished, run needle and floss under 4 or 5 stitches on back of design and trim tail close to fabric. Subsequent lengths of floss may be secured in same manner.

Stitching Method: For smooth stitches, use push-and-pull method. Starting on wrong side of fabric, bring needle straight up, pulling floss completely through to right side. Reinsert needle and bring it back straight down, pulling needle and floss completely through to back of fabric. Keep floss flat but do not pull thread tight. For even stitches, tension should be consistent throughout.

Carrying Floss: To carry floss, weave it under previously worked stitches on back of design. Do not carry floss across any fabric that is not or will not be stitched. Loose threads, especially dark ones, will show through fabric.

Cleaning Completed Work: When stitching is complete, soak finished piece in cold water with mild soap for 5 to 10 minutes. Rinse thoroughly. Roll work in towel to remove excess water. Do not wring. Place work face down on dry towel and press with warm iron until dry.

PLASTIC CANVAS

Plastic canvas is a molded, nonwoven material made from clear or colored plastic, consisting of "bars" with "holes" in between. It comes in mesh sizes 7, 10, and 14, which refer to number of holes per inch.

Always allow 2 empty grids outside stitched area. Keep floss tension even to ensure that each stitch lies flat and even. If floss is pulled too tight, canvas will show between stitches. If it is too loose, floss will not lie flat, causing bars of canvas to show.

Unless otherwise directed, the last step in color code for plastic canvas is cut and overcast step, indicated by thick black lines on graph. These lines show where to cut and overcast stitched piece. Read color code before overcasting.

Once a piece has been stitched, use sharp scissors to cut in space between 2 unstitched bars indicated on graph. Trim remaining nubs. Also cut all corners on the diagonal, but not so close that they weaken (Diagram A).

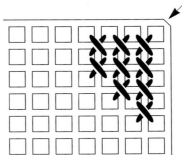

Diagram A

This makes overcasting edges easier (Diagram B). The overcast stitch is also used to join 2 or more pieces of plastic canvas. Align raw edges at required angle and work stitches to join those edges.

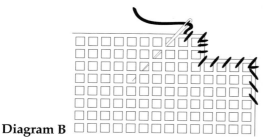

Diagram B

Hand-wash plastic canvas work in warm water with mild detergent. Do not scrub. Rinse thoroughly and air-dry. The heat of a clothes dryer may cause plastic canvas to melt. It cannot be dry-cleaned, either, because chemicals used will dissolve canvas.

WASTE CANVAS

Cut waste canvas 1" larger on all sides than finished design size. Baste waste canvas to fabric to be stitched. Each stitch is over 1 unit (2 threads). When stitching is complete, dampen stitched area with cold water. Pull waste canvas threads out 1 at a time with tweezers. It is easier to pull all threads running in 1 direction first; then pull out opposite threads. Allow stitching to dry; then place facedown on a towel and iron.

STITCHES

Cross-stitch: Make 1 cross-stitch for each symbol on chart. Bring needle up at A, down at B, up at C, and down again at D (Diagram C). For rows, stitch across fabric from left to right to make half-crosses and then back to complete stitch (Diagram D). All bottom half-crosses should slant in same direction; top half-crosses should slant in opposite direction.

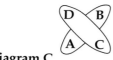

Diagram C

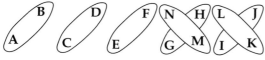

Diagram D

Three-quarter Stitch:
Three-quarter stitch is indicated on graph when a symbol fills only half of a square (Diagram E). If you are working over 1 thread, the short understitch will pierce fabric area; if you are working over 2 threads, it will slip through hole between 2 threads. In each case

the long stitch is the overstitch, even though in some cases this may violate the rule that all stitches should be worked from left to right and back again.

When 2 symbols occupy a single square on graph, make a three-quarter stitch and a quarter stitch to fill square. Which symbol applies to which stitch depends on the line you want to emphasize. Use three-quarter stitch to express dominant line or color (Diagram F).

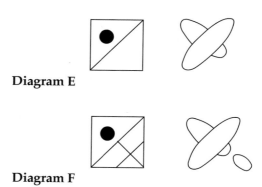

Diagram E

Diagram F

Backstitch: Complete all cross-stitches before working backstitches or other accent stitches. Working from right to left with 1 strand of floss (unless indicated otherwise in color code), bring needle up at A, down at B, and up at C. Going back down at A, continue in this manner (Diagram G).

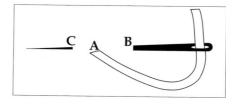

Diagram G

French Knot: Bring needle and floss up at A. Wrap floss around needle twice (unless indicated otherwise in color code). Insert needle beside A, pulling floss until it fits snugly around needle. Pull needle through to back (Diagram H).

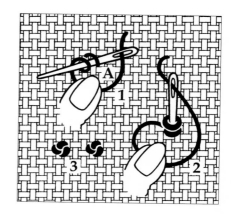

Diagram H

Beadwork: First, attach bead to fabric with diagonal stitch, from lower left to upper right. Secure bead by returning floss through bead, from lower right to upper left (Diagram I). When working in rows, complete a row of diagonal half-cross stitches before returning to secure all beads.

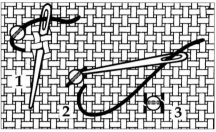

Diagram I

Kloster Blocks: To make a kloster block, work 5 satin stitches over 4 threads (Diagram J). The number of blocks will vary, depending on motif. Complete all kloster blocks in a motif before you begin cutting. Be sure that whatever their distance apart, each kloster block has another one exactly opposite (Diagram K). Before cutting any threads, check again that there are 2 kloster blocks opposite one another. Use sharp embroidery scissors with narrow tips. Insert scissors under 4 fabric threads next to satin stitches in that kloster block (Diagram K). Cut 4 threads close to satin stitches; then cut fabric threads next to satin stitches of opposite block. Cut only one area at a time. Cut ends visible at edges of kloster block will shrink behind when piece is washed.

Remove cut threads by gently pulling them out with tweezers. Avoid pulling fabric out of shape.

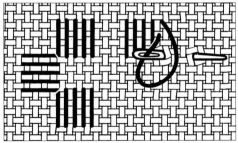

Diagram J

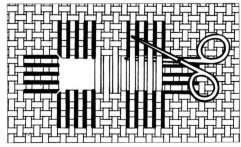

Diagram K

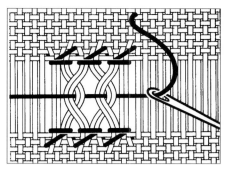

Twisted Ladder Hemstitch

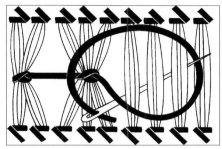

Triple Grouped Hemstitch

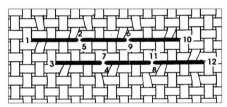

Faggot Stitch

TASSELS

You will need small scissors, a large-eyed tapestry needle, and a small piece of sturdy cardboard.

1. Winding: Cut a rectangle of cardboard ½" to 1" longer than desired length of finished tassel.

For a tassel made of thin fiber, cut an 8" strand of fiber and set aside. Wind remainder as many times as desired around length of cardboard (Diagram L). *Note:* For best results, lay strands side by side on cardboard, not on top of each other.

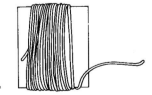

Diagram L

For a tassel made of fiber too thick to thread through a needle, cut an 8" strand and lay it across top edge of cardboard. Wind remainder as many times as desired around length of cardboard, over 8" strand.

2. Securing and Cutting: When the bundle of strands is wound to desired thickness, tie it at the top with a securing knot as follows. For a tassel made of thin fiber, thread a large-eyed needle with reserved 8" strand. Slide needle under 1 end of bundle of strands (Diagram M). Tie strand around bundle. For a tassel made of thick fiber, tie 8" strand at top edge of cardboard around bundle. Cut untied ends of strands at opposite edge of cardboard (Diagram N).

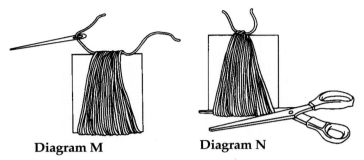

Diagram M   **Diagram N**

3. Finishing: About one-third of the way down from top of tassel, tightly wrap a 12" strand several times around bundle. Tie ends securely (Diagram O). Use a tapestry needle or crochet hook to hide loose ends of strand in tassel. Trim tassel to desired length.

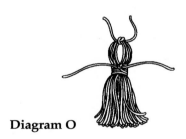

Diagram O

A second finishing method is the wrap knot. Form a narrow loop in 1 end of a 12" wrapping strand (Diagram P). Lay loop flat against tassel, with loop down and extending slightly below area to be wrapped (Diagram P). Evenly wrap strand around loop and bundle of strands until loop is almost covered. Insert end of wrapping strand through bottom of loop (Diagram Q). Pull opposite end of strand to hide loop within knot. Use a tapestry needle or crochet hook to hide loose end of wrapping strand into tassel. Trim tassel to desired length.

Diagram P   **Diagram Q**

Suppliers

All products are available retail from Shepherd's Bush, 220 24th Street, Ogden, UT 84401; (801) 399-4546. Or for a merchant near you, write or call the following suppliers:

Zweigart Fabrics—Zweigart/Joan Toggitt Ltd., Weston Canal Plaza, 2 Riverview Drive, Somerset, NJ 08873; (908) 271-1949

Zweigart Fabrics used:

Cream Aida 14	Cream Linda 27
Light Blue Aida 14	Moss Green Linen 30
Oatmeal Floba 18	Cream Belfast Linen 32
Pink Damask Aida 18	Driftwood Belfast Linen 32
Black Dublin 25	White Belfast Linen 32

Wichelt Fabrics—Wichelt Imports, Inc., Rural Route 1, Stoddard, WI 54648; (608) 788-4600

Wichelt Fabrics used:

Amber Linen 28	Champagne Linen 28
Antique Green Linen 28	English Rose Linen 28
Blush Linen 28	Shell Linen 28

Waste Canvas 14, Tea Linen 36—Charles Craft, P.O. Box 1049, Laurinburg, NC 28353; 1-800-277-0980

Glenshee Linen 29—Ann Powell Limited, P.O. Box 3060, Stuart, FL 34995; (407) 287-3007

Plastic Canvas 14, Vanessa-Ann Afghan Weave 18—Chapelle Designers, P.O. Box 9252, Newgate Station, Ogden, UT 84409; (801) 621-2777

DMC Floss, DMC Medicis, DMC Pearl Cotton—The DMC Corporation, Port Kearny, Building #10, South Kearny, NJ 07032; 1-800-688-8362

Overture Yarn—The Rainbow Gallery, 7412 Fulton Avenue 5, North Hollywood, CA 91605; 1-800-522-6827

Balger Blending Filament, Balger Gold Cord—Kreinik Mfg. Co., Inc., P.O. Box 1966, Parkersburg, WV 26101; 1-800-624-1928

Mill Hill Beads—Gay Bowles Sales, Inc., P.O. Box 1060, Janesville, WI 53547; (608) 754-9466

Crystal Jars—Anne Brinkley Designs, Inc., 761 Palmer Avenue, Holmdel, NJ 07733; 1-800-633-0148

Bellpull Hardware (Stock #121, Jyette)—Feldman Enterprises, 4215 Alta Vista Lane, Dallas, TX 75229; (214) 352-8695

Stuffing—Fairfield Processing Corporation, P.O. Box 1157, Danbury, CT 06813; 1-800-243-0989

Sewing Machine—Bernina of America, 3500 Thayer Court, Aurora, IL 60504-6182; (708) 978-2500

Ribbon—Offray and Son, Inc., 360 Route 24, Chester, NJ 07930; (908) 879-4700

Cover Design

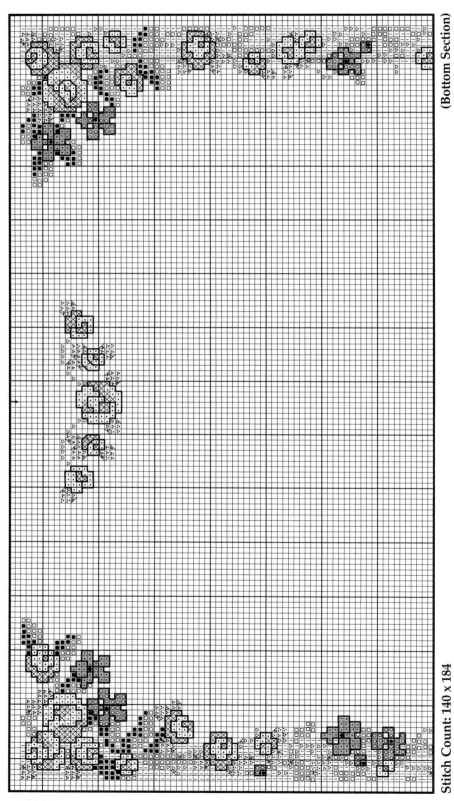

Stitch Count: 140 x 184

SAMPLE

Stitched on cream Belfast Linen 32 over 2 threads, the finished design size is 8¾" x 11½". The fabric was cut 15" x 18".

FABRICS	DESIGN SIZES
Aida 11	12¾" x 16¾"
Aida 14	10" x 13⅛"
Aida 18	7¾" x 10¼"
Hardanger 22	6⅜" x 8⅜"

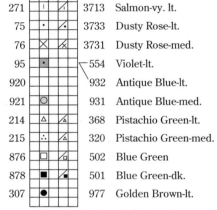

Anchor			DMC (used for sample)	
Step 1: Cross-stitch (2 strands)				
271	I	⁄	3713	Salmon-vy. lt.
75	·	⁄	3733	Dusty Rose-lt.
76	X	⁄	3731	Dusty Rose-med.
95	▨		554	Violet-lt.
920			932	Antique Blue-lt.
921	○		931	Antique Blue-med.
214	△	⁄	368	Pistachio Green-lt.
215	∴	⁄	320	Pistachio Green-med.
876	□	⁄	502	Blue Green
878	■	⁄	501	Blue Green-dk.
307	●		977	Golden Brown-lt.
Step 2: Backstitch (1 strand)				
42			3350	Dusty Rose-dk. (pink flowers)
922			930	Antique Blue-dk. (blue flowers)

144